John A. Simpson

Confederate veteran

John A. Simpson

Confederate veteran

ISBN/EAN: 9783741146206

Manufactured in Europe, USA, Canada, Australia, Japa

Cover: Foto ©Thomas Meinert / pixelio.de

Manufactured and distributed by brebook publishing software
(www.brebook.com)

John A. Simpson

Confederate veteran

VOL. XXV.   **FEBRUARY, 1917**   **NO. 2**

JUDGE J. A. P. CAMPBELL, OF MISSISSIPPI
Member of the First Provisional Congress of the Southern Confederacy and
one of the signers of the Confederate Constitution. (See page 54.)

Confederate Veteran.

PUBLISHED MONTHLY IN THE INTEREST OF CONFEDERATE ASSOCIATIONS AND KINDRED TOPICS.

Entered at the post office at Nashville, Tenn., as second-class matter.
Date given to subscription is the month of expiration.
All remittances should be made to the CONFEDERATE VETERAN,
and all communications so addressed.
Published by the Confederate Veteran Company, Nashville, Tenn.

OFFICIALLY REPRESENTS:
UNITED CONFEDERATE VETERANS,
UNITED DAUGHTERS OF THE CONFEDERACY,
SONS OF VETERANS AND OTHER ORGANIZATIONS,
CONFEDERATED SOUTHERN MEMORIAL ASSOCIATION.

Though men deserve, they may not win, success;
The brave will honor the brave, vanquished none the less.

PRICE, $1.00 PER YEAR.
SINGLE COPY, 10 CENTS.
VOL. XXV. NASHVILLE, TENN., FEBRUARY, 1917. No. 2. S. A. CUNNINGHAM, FOUNDER.

REUNION ORDERS.

HEADQUARTERS UNITED CONFEDERATE VETERANS.
NEW ORLEANS, LA., January 15, 1917.

GENERAL ORDERS No. 6.

I. The twenty-seventh annual Reunion of the United Confederate Veterans will be held in Washington, D. C., June 5, 6, and 7, 1917. This date has been agreed upon by the Commander in Chief and three Department Commanders and fixed at the suggestion as well as with the full approval of the local committee charged with the management of the details of the meeting.

These are the days set aside for the transaction of the business of the Association; but the good people of Washington have arranged for such pleasures and entertainments as will take up the entire week, commencing the fourth day of June.

This is the first time a Reunion has taken place outside of the limits of the late Confederate States, and it is eminently fit that it should be held in the city of Washington.

"On to Washington! On to Washington!" was the cry of Confederate soldiers after the victory of the First Manassas; but the judgment of the leaders was averse to the movement. Furthermore, the trenches near the city were defended by a line of men in blue, ready to dispute any attempt on the part of the Confederates to enter their territory. "On to Washington! On to Washington!" is shouted again throughout the Southland, and now the leaders cheerfully urge their commands forward, while the opposing blues, instead of making any objection, welcome with cordial handshake their late foes. These men, with the citizens in general of the capital city of the country, promise that this gathering shall in every respect be the most memorable in the history of the United Confederate Veterans.

It was a beautiful, pathetic, and patriotic act on the part of the local G. A. R. Post to take the initiative in asking that this Reunion be held in Washington, and it is one which fills the hearts of the Confederate soldiers with heartiest pleasure and shows to the world that the United States are one country, with one flag and one aim.

The General commanding notes with sincere satisfaction the great efforts the committees in Washington are making for the entertainment of the men whom it is his privilege to command, and he can promise his comrades that no efforts will be spared, no outlay curtailed to add to the pleasure of the old Confederates.

To march down Pennsylvania Avenue in full uniform, to be reviewed by the President of the United States, surrounded by all the foreign dignitaries in Washington—this should arouse the enthusiasm of the most callous and add to the attendance from the entire South. The General commanding urges every one to attend this great assembly, which promises to be one of the most notable events in American history, long to live in the memory of every one who is present and who will be proud to say: "I was at the Confederate Reunion in Washington."

II. It is particularly desired that members of Camps attend in uniform. These uniforms can be had at reasonable prices, and Col. N. B. Forrest, of Biloxi, Miss., with enviable energy and devotion, has done much work to bring about these low prices. Officers should at once take up this matter with him.

III. The General commanding with much pleasure announces, at the request of its most energetic President, Mrs. W. J. Behan, that the Confederated Southern Memorial Association will hold its meeting at the same time, and the Sons of Confederate Veterans will hold their convention on the same days.

IV. The monument erected by the State of Virginia to the memory of her soldiers at Gettysburg will be unveiled on June 8 or 9 on the battle field. This date has been fixed by the Virginia Commission so that the veterans may easily go from Washington. Arrangements will be made with the railroads to handle passengers from Washington to Gettysburg and return. This will be a most important event, and it is hoped by the General commanding that as many as possible of the veterans will make arrangements to attend.

V. The General commanding sincerely hopes that the press of the entire country, ever ready to promote the cause of the Confederate soldier, will endeavor to stir up interest in the coming meeting, and to this end he requests that this order be published and editorial comment made thereon.

By command of GEORGE P. HARRISON.
General Commanding.
WM. E. MICKLE, *Adjutant General and Chief of Staff.*

PORTRAITS OF GENERAL LEE.

"Yet when I view your old-time picture all
The proud past rises, though its day is fled."

One of the latest biographers of General Lee makes a comparison of his pictures in early and late life, in which he says: "From the study of photographs I get a more charming impression of his later years than of his earlier. The face and figure of the captain are eminently noble, high-bred, dignified; but with the dignity there is just a suggestion of haughtiness, of remoteness. But in the bearded photographs of later years all traces of such remoteness have vanished. The dignity is more marked than ever, but all sweet. The ample, lordly carriage, the broad brow, the deep, significant, intelligent eyes convey nothing but the largest tenderness, the profoundest human sympathy, the most perfect love."

We can concur in this impression of General Lee in his maturity, but who that has read of his gentle youth and

CAPT. R. E. LEE, U. S. ENGINEERS.

thoughtful manhood can associate with him any idea of haughtiness or other quality that would in the least repel? True, there was about him that remoteness which made him seem almost as a man set apart by God for some high and lofty purpose, yet it but ennobles the countenance in giving the impression as of one who had to tread the way of life alone.

General Lee's son, Capt. R. E. Lee, Jr., in referring to a certain portrait considered a good likeness, said: "To me the expression of strength peculiar to his face is wanting, and the mouth fails to portray that sweetness of disposition so characteristic of his countenance. * * * My father never could bear to have his picture taken, and there are no likenesses of him that really give his sweet expression."

The picture of General Lee with which we are most familiar is the gray-bearded man with the dignified yet kindly mien which gives the impression of strength of character above all things. But there is an appeal about all his pictured representations. One can imagine his mother's joy in his physical perfectness as well as in that spiritual tenderness which made him both a son and daughter to her.

It is said that General Lee was the embodiment of manly beauty, of "a noble and commanding presence and an admirable, graceful, and athletic figure." At the time he became Superintendent at West Point he was pictured as tall and erect, with wavy black hair, hazel-brown eyes, and "a countenance which beamed with gentleness and intelligence." General Hunt described him as "fine-looking a man as one would wish to see, of perfect figure, and strikingly handsome." Another writes of the impression made at the time of the war, when more years had passed over him: "His form had full-

ness without any appearance of superfluous flesh, as erect as that of a cadet. * * * No representation of General Lee properly conveys the light and softness of his eye. the tenderness and intelligence of his mouth. or the indescribable refinement of his face." And Alexander H. Stephens, when he saw Robert E. Lee for the first time and pressed upon him the question of Virginia's joining the Confederacy, felt that he was well worthy to make a great decision in a great cause. "As he stood there," said Mr. Stephens, "fresh and ruddy as a David from the sheepfold. in the prime of manly beauty,

GEN. R. E. LEE, C. S. A.

and the embodiment of a line of heroic and patriotic fathers and worthy mothers —it was thus I first saw Robert E. Lee. * * * I had before me the most manly and entire gentleman I ever saw."

Thus in the prime of his strength and manly excellence he entered the war of secession, and by the record of his pictures we trace the progress of age, not of years, but that which comes from the weight of responsibility, from the burden of sorrow, and from the crushing realization of failure. Yet through it all the countenance never loses that serenity, that sweetness of noble dignity which made him kingly among men.

THE HAMPTON ROADS CONFERENCE.

In the preparation of his article on the Hampton Roads Conference of February 3, 1865, Gen. Julian S. Carr, of North Carolina, has rendered a great service to history. Although this matter was brought out at length in the VETERAN for June and July, 1916, the false statements have continued to be circulated; but it is hoped that General Carr's exhaustive treatment of the subject will be effective in silencing the disseminators of such statements. No one can read the article without realizing that he has demonstrated the falsity of the statement regarding a proposition by President Lincoln to Hon. Alexander H. Stephens, and every Confederate and others who are interested in the truth of history will feel a sense of obligation to General Carr for the splendid work he has done in demonstrating for all time that the story is a fiction, having no foundation except in the imagination of those who desire to glorify Mr. Lincoln. (See page 57.)

THE JEFFERSON DAVIS MEMORIAL AT FAIRVIEW.

On page 67 of this number appears the address made by Gen. Bennett H. Young to the Daughters of the Confederacy in convention at Dallas, Tex., November 10, 1916, on the memorial to be erected to Jefferson Davis, only President of the Southern Confederacy, at Fairview, Ky. The splendid liberality of Gens. George W. Littlefield, of Texas, and

(Continued on page 99.)

Confederate Veteran.

THE HOUSE WHERE STONEWALL JACKSON DIED.

BY EMMA FRANCES LEE SMITH.

'Mid fair Virginia's gently swelling plains,
  Where once the roar of battle shook the hills,
Unique amongst all consecrated fanes,
  Quaint with a beauty that inspires and thrills,

There stands a little house with roof tree low
  And white walls gleaming 'neath the summer skies.
By what swift magic does it bring the glow
  Of reverent wonder to our eager eyes?

"Whose is that humble cot?" I asked of one,
  And with a glance of ardor he replied
In the soft speech that marks the Southland's son:
  "That is the house where Stonewall Jackson died."

Then I bethought me of that mournful day
  When over all this smiling, happy land
The darkness of a tragic sorrow lay
  As Stonewall's sword fell from his stricken hand.

When from the field they bore their hero chief,
  His blood-stained warriors wept with bitter rage;
His dying eyes saw through the mirk of grief
  Green trees of heav'n with verdant foliage.

"Let us pass over the river," he sighed,
  "And rest under the shade, the shade of the trees."
As he had lived, most valiantly he died
  With childlike faith in God's divine decrees.

In vain we questioned through the long, sad years
  Why the just God of battles willed it so,
And heeded not the anguish and the tears
  And the sick hearts that shrank beneath that blow.

But as the smoke of conflict cleared away
  And sweet-browed peace came with her message blest,
Slowly we learned to lift our eyes and say:
  "Thy way, O God, not ours, for thine is best."

So, little house beside the dusty road,
  Cherish for aye the memory and the pride
So strangely by an unseen Power bestowed—
  Dear little house, where Stonewall Jackson died.

.THE HOUSE WHERE JACKSON DIED.

MISS KATE MASON ROWLAND.

BY DR. HENRY E. SHEPHERD, BALTIMORE, MD.

I noted not merely with surprise, but with a feeling approaching to chagrin and mortification, that in the tributes to their dead of 1916 by the United Daughters of the Confederacy at their recent convention in Dallas, Tex., the name of the most cultured, brilliant, and heroic woman ever associated with the history of the South is passed over in absolute silence.

Miss Kate Mason Rowland, of Virginia, who died in Richmond, Va., June 29, 1916, illustrated the ideal type of Southern womanhood as it prevailed in the days that are dead—and the charms and graces of a historic lineage, with comprehensive and catholic acquirement, uncompromising and invincible allegiance to the aims and aspirations embodied in the cause of the Confederacy. She was a collateral descendant of George Mason, of Gunston Hall, the friend of Washington and author of the Virginia Bill of Rights. Her "Life of Mason" and of "Charles Carroll, of Carrollton," have long since attained the rank of classics. In addition to these, her edition of the poems of Dr. Ticknor and "The Journal of Julie LeGrand" reveal the same finely touched literary discrimination characteristic of her work in the sphere of biography. I have more than once compared Miss Rowland to Flora McIvor, the heroine of Scott's "Waverly." In either case life and energy, mind and heart were consecrated to a single purpose, and in each instance the dream faded, the vision of the house of Stuart as well as the "Ethnogenesis" of our fadeless Southern lyrist. During her final illness, when almost in "the twilight of eternal day," Miss Rowland wrote me that she trusted I might be spared to bestow a few more whacks upon certain Southern recreants "who, like Sir Bedivere, had betrayed their nature and their names."

In her life and character devotion, unswerving fidelity, and singleness of aim blended into harmony with purity and range of attainment in the high realms of literature and history. Yet in the official report of the dead for 1916 her record is passed over by her colaborers and sisters as though she had never been.

PATRIOTISM OF MISSISSIPPI WOMEN.

The legislature of Mississippi recognized the devotion and loyalty of the women of the State to the cause in the following resolution adopted January 28, 1862: "That the women of the State of Mississippi, for their exertions in behalf of the cause of Southern independence, are entitled to the hearty thanks of every lover of his country; and this legislature, acting from a sense of justice and gratitude, extends to them, individually and collectively, the sincere thanks of the people of this State for their noble efforts in aiding the cause of our common country."

In his inaugural address to the legislature on November 16, 1863, on this subject Governor Clark said: "One of the most gratifying indications of the times is the resolute spirit of industry manifested by our women. The spinning wheel is preferred to the harp, and the loom makes music of loftier patriotism and inspiration than the keys of the piano."

The strength of the Confederacy was largely in the heroic devotion and patriotic self-sacrifice of the women of the South, and it is gratifying to know that this was freely recognized and appreciated at the time by such official acts. The women of all the other Southern States were no less industrious and devoted to the cause.

2*

APPOMATTOX, APRIL 9, 1865.

BY B. W. J., SPOTTSVILLE, VA.

On mem'ry's bell I hear again
  The echoes of that direful day,
When valor owned the struggle vain
  And threw the well-worn sword away.

Our chieftain's eagle eye was dim;
  His heart was sad, his words were brief,
And tearful orbs were turned to him
  That seldom wept o'er private grief.

Upon the field the soldier laid
  The arms he knew how well to bear,
But o'er his brow a shadow strayed,
  For long-tried friends were severed there.

He turned to go, but paused in shame
  That this must be the end at last
And fearing much lest on his name
  The coward's stigma should be cast.

But hark! the cannon's sullen roar
  Again disturbs the morning air,
The old defiance telling o'er
  That warns the foe brave men are there.

Now back unto their guns they spring;
  The fire of hope has blazed anew;
Quick to the breeze their flags they fling,
  While armed battalions rise to view.

Alas! 'tis vain. Across the field
  A horseman speeds with message dire.
The South to fate the cause must yield
  And see her cherished aims expire.

Ah, woeful day! A nation died
  When Lee that vernal morning laid
His chieftain's armor all aside,
  No more to wield the warrior's blade.

Ah, direful fate! But future years
  Will bring the gift we fought to gain,
For all this blood and all these tears
  Were never meant to flow in vain.

Above our dead to-day we lay
  The cypress wreath to mark their graves.
When time shall bring our natal day,
  We'll reckon them our conq'ring braves.

THAT APPLE TREE AT APPOMATTOX.

BY J. C. REED, HAMPTON, VA.

I have read with great interest the article in the January VETERAN concerning the "Historic Apple Tree at Appomattox." Having a more perfect knowledge of that noted apple tree, I here record the facts. When the surrender took place, I was a sergeant in the Bedford Light Artillery, Hager's Battalion, Longstreet's Corps. Capt. John Donnell Smith commanded the battery.

After the surrender our guns were parked near a log dwelling which is still standing. That dwelling was on a ridge, in front of which, about twenty-five or thirty yards, there was a small branch, or ditch. Just beyond this ditch, about thirty yards away, was the famous apple tree. My tent was pitched on this branch on the side next to the dwelling spoken of and was therefore about midway between the house and the tree. We remained in this place several days while our paroles were being prepared.

The apple tree was not destroyed by the Confederates. Many small twigs and limbs were broken off by the Confederate soldiers. I myself broke off two small twigs and put them in my pocketbook and carried them home. I can bear witness that the tree did disappear one night. It was either on Tuesday or Wednesday night. I do not know, but I feel sure that some enterprising Yankee cut it down and carried it away. I know that I went to sleep with the tree within thirty yards of my tent, and the next morning it was gone. I suspect that a thousand souvenirs of apple tree wood have been sold claimed to be a part of that tree.

The present marker, whose inscription is given on the front cover of the VETERAN for January, I have often seen. It stands near the road and about four hundred yards from where the apple tree stood. I feel confident, were I permitted to do so, that I could place that marker within a few feet of the original site of the tree.

THE ANNE LEE MEMORIAL.

[In an address before the Virginia State Convention, U. D. C., at Lynchburg on October 10, 1916, Mrs. Lycurgus Edward Uhler eloquently set forth the plans for the Anne Lee Memorial Home for the Aged as a tribute to the memory of General Lee's mother. No finer tribute could be paid to General Lee and his mother than to dedicate this old home in Alexandria to the aged women who sacrificed and suffered for the Southern cause. Every Southern man and woman should be glad to honor General Lee by contributing to the memorial to his mother. There are now in the Home three widows of Confederate veterans, and others will soon be admitted. There is need of your coöperation in sustaining this work. All contributions should be sent to Mrs. Uhler, who is Vice President of the Association and also Chairman of the Finance Committee. Address her at 321 Washington Street, Alexandria, Va.]

A subject which must appeal to every Southern woman is the memorial to Anne Carter Lee, the mother of Virginia's illustrious soldier and statesman, Gen. Robert Edward Lee, whose brave deeds, noble patriotism, and honorable record won for him undying fame and the love and devotion of a grateful Confederacy. Of his mother General Lee once said, "All I am I owe to my mother"; and Gen. Fitzhugh Lee writes of her: "I have always heard that to her noble influence the perfect formation of General Lee's character was due." Thus to Anne Carter Lee the South owes her illustrious leader.

The first memorial erected by women to a woman was that to Mary the mother of Washington, and every Southern man and woman must feel that the second should be to the memory of the mother of Gen. Robert E. Lee, Virginia's noble chieftain.

About seventeen years ago the women of Alexandria, moved by a desire to commemorate the virtues of the mother of our beloved general, formed an association, the "Anne Lee Memorial Association." Its President was Mrs. L. Wilbur Reid, now President of the Seventeenth Virginia Regiment Chapter, U. D. C. Sufficient funds not being secured at that time for a suitable memorial, the money was invested; and in March, 1915, the work was again taken up, a board of governers was elected, and plans formed to make the memorial a home for the aged.

No more suitable place for this memorial could be selected than Alexandria. Anne Lee's home was there; she was a member of Old Christ Church, and but a few miles away, at Ravensworth, her remains lie buried. There could be no

HOME OF GENERAL LEE'S MOTHER, IN ALEXANDRIA, VA.
The building is in colonial yellow, with white trimmings.

more beautiful tribute to her memory than the care of the aged without home and loved ones to brighten their few remaining years.

It was in Alexandria in the yard of Old Christ Church, of which he was at that time a member and vestryman, that General Lee announced his determination to cast his lot with his native State in the pending conflict, stating his purpose to leave the next day to join the army of the Confederacy and offer his sword in defense of his native State.

We have purchased the old colonial home of the Herbert family, in the historic section of our city, within a few steps of the Carlyle House, Braddock House, and General Washington's headquarters, ideal for our purpose, with wonderful possibilities, but very much out of repair. When all improvements are completed, we will accommodate twenty to twenty-five inmates.

The Seventeenth Virginia Regiment Chapter, through the untiring energy of our President, Mrs. Reid, has erected a colonial portico and entrance at a cost of $700, and on the ground floor is a beautifully furnished reception room, also a gift of the Seventeenth Chapter. Checks have been sent to the chairman of the Finance Committee from the New York Chapter; the Mary Mildred Sullivan Chapter, of New York; the Dixie Club, of New York; the Maryland Chapter, of Baltimore; and the Fairfax Chapter, of Fairfax. And we most earnestly solicit the coöperation of every Chapter in raising a fund to make a memorial the South can point to with pride.

In addition to the patriotic sentiment, it is a feeling of tenderness for the pitiful condition of a number of old wom-

en, several of them widows of Confederate veterans, that prompted us to devise a means to care for these dear old people. I have found that in almost every city there is crying need of a home for a class of women who by birth and education are unfitted for the ordinary charitable institutions. I could give you several examples among applicants for admission to our home; women who a few years ago were surrounded by every luxury wealth could devise or heart desire, but who to-day through misfortune or the passing away of loved ones are suffering abject poverty.

It is hard for youth to battle through life against poverty, but they have a future before them, something to hope for, something to work for; but our aged, what have they but memories! How true it is that "sorrow's crown of sorrows is remembering happier things"!

It was truly a brave undertaking; and while the country has been drained to send help to those suffering from the terrors of the gruesome war, we have raised over $5,000. We should be congratulated on the work we have achieved under the existing conditions; but so thoroughly understood is the feeling that our tenderest consideration should be for the aged that, it matters not what urgent needs develop, when the time and call for contributions arrive the care of the aged has the first claim on our hearts and purses.

Our work has progressed despite the wave of financial depression which has swept our country, but the time has come when we ask assistance from our Daughters. We need $4,000 to finish our improvements, put in our lights and heating plant, and we beg you whose religion is founded on charity and patriotism to give us a helping hand to aid us to complete our memorial. And as the shadows of little day in which these dear old people are now sojourning lengthen out toward the most perfect day to which they are fast approaching and the eventide of life's brief journey is gathering its gray mists around them help us, who regard it as a blessed privilege to guide with loving care their weary footsteps to the threshold of that door which sooner or later will open for us all.

It is our wish and hope that U. D. C. Chapters will furnish and endow for $1,000 the room on the ground floor adjoining the Seventeenth Virginia Regiment Chapter room, to be used for the widow or daughter of a veteran who can be sent to us from any part of Virginia.

Our home is paid for; we have no debt, and up to this time $1,500 has been paid for improvements, and we are incorporated under the State laws of Virginia.

It is not our wish to make the Anne Lee Memorial Home for the Aged a local institution; it should be a memorial made by Southern women. And we appeal not only to U. D. C. Chapters, but to every Southern woman individually to give $1 (or more) to an endowment fund. We feel so fully assured of your sympathy and interest that we are satisfied we shall not ask in vain. We trust that our Daughters as a whole will respond with widespread enthusiasm to this appeal. Do not let us feel that outside interest is greater than ours.

In conclusion, let me say in regard to personal donation, as this home is a memorial to a mother, make your gift to us in the name of your own mother. She may still be with you, guarded by your tender love and care, or she may have passed on to the beyond, leaving in your hearts a heritage of loving memories. Keep the holiness of the Anne Lee Memorial work ever before you, and let each and every one give as best he can to the earnest workers who are striving to fulfill our dear Lord's teaching in caring for his children.

LAST SURVIVOR OF THE ORIGINAL CON-
FEDERATE STATES CONGRESS.

In the fullness of years, Judge J. A. P. Campbell, eminent jurist of Mississippi, died at his home, in Jackson, Miss., on January 10, 1917. He had reached the ripe age of eighty-seven years.

Of the forty-nine members of the first Provisional Congress of the seceding States meeting at Montgomery, Ala., in February, 1861, there is now not a survivor. The death of Judge Campbell marks the passing of the last of this famous body of men sent by the States of Alabama, Mississippi, Georgia, South Carolina, Florida, Louisiana, and Texas to organize the Confederate government and the last of the signers of the Confederate Constitution. He was only thirty-one when appointed a member of the delegation sent by Mississippi, youngest of the seven representatives of that State and also the youngest member of that Congress.

Josiah A. P. Campbell was born in South Carolina March 2, 1830, and went to Madison County, Miss., with his parents in 1845. His father was a well-known Presbyterian minister, a graduate of Princeton University. From his earliest years the son seemed to have a natural aptitude for the law, and he became a close student of the profession, beginning his practice at Kosciusko in 1847 when but seventeen years of age. At twenty-one he was elected to the State legislature, and five years later he was Speaker of the House of Representatives. He was also serving in that capacity in 1861 when the question of secession aroused the Southland. As one of the leaders in affairs of State, he was a member of the Constitutional Convention of Mississippi which adopted the ordinance of secession, and his appointment as one of the delegates sent by that State to the first constitutional convention of the Confederacy naturally followed. His associates were Wiley P. Harris, W. S. Wilson, Walker Brooke, A. M. Clayton, W. S. Barry, and James T. Harrison.

Some years ago, in reminiscing on the Confederacy's birth, Judge Campbell referred to the Congress as "a very able body of men, as the States had as a rule selected leaders to represent them on that occasion." He further said: "I cannot recall all the members representing the six States that participated, but some of them stand out to my mind's eye now with wonderful clearness and distinctness. The South Carolina delegation was led by Robert Barnwell Rhett, a very able man, with a list of strong associates. Toombs, Stephens, and Cobb stood out conspicuously among the Georgians. Louisiana had Judah P. Benjamin; Conrad, himself an ex-Secretary of War; Slidell, Kenner, Sparrow, and others whom I do not at this moment recall. J. L. M. Curry was of the Alabama delegation."

After the organization of the Confederate government, Judge Campbell returned to Mississippi and took up arms for his State, serving as captain, lieutenant colonel, and colonel. As lieutenant colonel of the 40th Mississippi he led that regiment in the battles of Shiloh, Iuka, and in other engagements and activities along the Tennessee Valley. He was severely wounded during his service and after recovering became a member of the judicial arm of the struggling Confederacy, and so continued until the surrender at Appomattox.

Going back to his State, full of energy and determination, he again built up his law practice. In 1865 he was elected judge of the fifth circuit district; but in the next year, during the régime of carpetbaggery, he refused to take the oath of renunciation, so left the bench and resumed his law practice, in which he later became associated with Judge S. S. Cal-

houn until 1884, when he was appointed as a member of the Supreme Court of Mississippi by Governor Stone. It was here that Judge Campbell rendered his most conspicuous public service. During the sixteen years he was on the supreme bench he was absent from his post only fourteen days. He was considered one of the soundest lawyers of the State and

HON. J. A. P. CAMPBELL, 1861.

was one of the three commissioners appointed to codify the statutes of Mississippi in 1870, and in 1878 he prepared a new legislative code of nearly two hundred sections. He was the acknowledged head of the Mississippi bar, the most clear-law giver and law adviser within the State, and to him many lawyers, judges, and practitioners turned for enlightenment through the medium of his ripe and conservative judgment and counsel.

In honor of this distinguished citizen the State offices were closed and the Capitol draped in mourning, while the schools of Jackson were suspended for half a day. The body of Judge Campbell lay in state in the rotunda of the Capitol until the hour of the funeral, hundreds of friends and relatives and other citizens of neighboring towns looking for the last time upon the face of the "Grand Old Man of Mississippi," as he was deservedly referred to. Many handsome floral designs were banked about the casket and hall. The funeral services were held at the First Baptist Church, of which Judge Campbell had been a member for many years. The honorary pall-bearers were members of R. A. Smith Camp, U. C. V., and of the bench and bar of Mississippi, while the active pall-bearers were his grandsons.

In 1850, shortly after he was twenty years old, Judge Campbell was married to Miss Eugenia Nash, and they lived happily together for fifty-six years. Five sons and three daughters were born to them, of whom two sons and two daughters survive: Robert B. Campbell, of Greenville, Miss.; Newton N. Campbell, of Greenville, Tex.; Mrs. Minnie Dameron, with whom he lived; and Mrs. Edward Yerger, of Jackson.

A NOTED LAW CLASS OF THE UNIVERSITY OF VIRGINIA.

[The annual address by Col. W. Gordon McCabe before the Virginia Historical Society as its President on March 20, 1916, contained a tribute to the late Judge Theodore S. Garnett, whose death occurred in April, 1915. In reviewing the life of this friend and comrade, Colonel McCabe tells of his entering the law school of the University of Virginia just after the war, sustained by the meager fund which his immediate family could supply, and he takes occasion to refer to the personnel of the class in which Judge Garnett was one of many who became distinguished in their life work.]

And just here it is not only pertinent, but indeed necessary even in so slight a sketch as this, that we should pause and consider the unique conditions that existed at the university during the two sessions—1865-66 and 1866-67—when Garnett was attending lectures there in the law school. To essay this may seem to some an irrelevant excursus, but this is far from true. We must know something of his environment during those years that ushered in his formal manhood if we would know the man himself.

As the conditions that existed were unique, equally unique was the "atmosphere" they created—an atmosphere which the youthful student drank in with full lungs and which inspired in him those lofty ideals as to the conduct of life that were to inform well-nigh every act and utterance of his maturer years. Never before and never since have there been two such sessions in the history of the great institution which is the pride of the commonwealth and of the whole South. It was a veritable era of "plain living and high thinking." The State harried by four years of devastating war, lay prostrate and could extend but meager help to "the child of Jefferson's old age." Everywhere were the outward signs of what is called "poverty," but it was the poverty which the great Greek tragedian in a well-known fragment calls "the stern parent who breeds the more strenuous sons better fitted for the strife of life." Beside such poverty, the "pauperies nitida" of the Roman poet, the smug luxury of the rich foundations of this commercial age seems mean and tawdry.

Never was there gathered within "the well-remembered gates of Alma Mater" such a band of determined students, a very large proportion of them, though young in years, veterans of Lee's army, who every day went to class in their faded old uniforms, making merry over the silly order of the military satrap who at the time reigned over "District No. 1," as "the mother of presidents" was then designated, requiring them and all other old soldiers to cover carefully the military buttons on their "fighting jackets." Richard Creur de Lion was still "in every bush." No doubt the "district commander," they soliloquized, was an ass to descend to such pettiness, but let it go; as for themselves, they had no time to give to him and his covering of buttons.

The perils and privations they had undergone had sobered them beyond their years; yet withal they were a cheerful set, full of health and vigor, save in a few cases, and touched with a natural exaltation at the thought that they had done their duty as good soldiers, as was attested by the many honorable wounds they could count among them; that they had stuck to "Ole Mars Robert" to the last and "seen the thing through"; and now here they were, safe and sound, with still a fighting chance to retrieve in some measure the educational sacrifices they had cheerfully made for hearth and home and country.

Optimism disdained to "consider too curiously" the very palpable *res angusta*. They wanted so little that they felt they still had much. Even if things were ill to-day, it should not be so to-morrow. Hadn't Horace said the identical thing nearly two thousand years ago?

"Non si male nunc, et olim
Sic erit."

And so they buckled afresh to their tasks with hearts as high as when they charged with Stuart at Aldie or went up the slopes of Cemetery Ridge.

Never before was the tie so close between professors and students, for it was the tie of comradeship, than which none on earth is stronger. The professorial staff was, indeed, small, but it was of the first order. Many of its members had been trained in the best universities at home and abroad, and, fired by unselfish devotion to their State and a proper pride in their calling, they gave without stint the best that was in them to their pupils, quite content to share the common lack and to labor for the most meager stipend.

Some changes had come about in the personnel of the faculty since the university had practically closed its doors in '62 and been turned into a hospital, but they were not many.

Albert Taylor Bledsoe, professor of mathematics, who had been at West Point with Jefferson Davis and been appointed by him at the outbreak of hostilities Assistant Secretary of War, had, it is true, resigned his chair and gone his way to Baltimore to edit the Southern Review and to write his famous book, "Is Davis a Traitor?" which carried consternation into the ranks of radical demagogues, who had been clamoring for President Davis's blood, and which by its inexorable logic and wealth of constitutional learning drove the reluctant law officers of the government to advise the dismissal of the indictments against the Confederate executive. Mr. Davis was never tried, because the Federal government was afraid to try him.

But Bledsoe's chair had been taken by Col. Charles Scott Venable, a brilliant mathematician trained in Germany, whose martial face and figure were familiar on every battle field to old soldiers, who knew him as one of Lee's most alert and daring staff officers.

Lewis Minor Coleman, professor of Latin, the gentle scholar, whom some of us—the lingering few—still hold fast in our "heart of hearts," had fallen mortally wounded amid his blackened guns in the moment of victory on the snow-clad heights of Fredericksburg, lieutenant colonel of the 1st Virginia Artillery; but in his place came in '66 William E. Peters, also trained in Germany, who as colonel of the 21st Virginia Cavalry had fallen desperately wounded in the fierce cavalry combat at Moorefield and been left for dead on that sanguinary field.

Yet another there is of these fighting professors who should find mention here, Basil L. Gildersleeve, now of the Johns-Hopkins University, the greatest Grecian of our time and one of the greatest scholars of any time, long since so recognized both in Germany and in England, who, still limping heavily from the grievous wound received in the Valley while serving on John B. Gordon's staff, might be seen daily making his way to his lecture room, where he expounded more brilliantly than ever to his eager class out of his own experiences in the field the varying fortunes of the Peloponnesian War as set down in the matchless pages of Thucydides, elucidating many a puzzling bit of strategy by apt illustrations drawn from the recent contest, in which professor and pupils had alike borne honorable part as tried comrades. Not seldom, too, would this great scholar relax for a brief space his inexorable syntactical grilling and enliven the close of the lecture hour by reading aloud (the reading punctured by tumultuous applause) his own exquisite and inspiring translations of the marching songs of Tyrtæus, the rush of whose swift anapests recalled to his delighted hearers the lilt of their own war songs, which they had sung, it seemed, but yesterday to the rhythmic beat of tramping feet as they swung down the Valley Pike under old Stonewall.

Others among the instructors had also served their State in arms, but we may not pause longer to make mention of them.

In the law class with Garnett what a bede roll had we but time to call it!

John W. Daniel, still on his crutches (as he was to the last day of his brilliant career) from the frightful wound he had received at the Wilderness in 1864, and Thomas S. Martin, who, too young to enter the army until the last year of the war, had yet seen active service in the Cadet Corps of the Virginia Military Institute, sat beside him on the rude wooden benches, both of them destined to represent Virginia for many years in the Senate of the United States. There too, of scarcely less note in after years, sat the brilliant Upshur Dennis, of Maryland, Lunsford Lomax Lewis, of Rockingham (afterwards on the bench of the Supreme Court of Virginia), and Edward Christian Minor, who had lost his arm in a cavalry skirmish at Luray in the Valley—all destined to become judges of note who did honor to the ermine.

Other future judges there were among these classmates of Garnett's, who himself became judge, and, in addition, a surprising number of men who in after years attained notable distinction in their profession, among them William H. White, who, be it noted, had taken part as a Virginia Military Institute cadet in the thrice-glorious battle of Newmarket and who became later on Garnett's law partner in a firm whose high reputation extended far beyond the boundaries of their native State.

One cannot resist the temptation to set down here that his most intimate friend (not, however, in the law school) was the late Joseph Bryan, so long the beloved president of this society, his old chum at the Episcopal High School, who had been twice wounded while serving as a simple trooper under the dashing Mosby. Another of these intimates, also in the Academic Department, was the lovable and talented Frank Preston, of Lexington, who, like Minor, had lost an arm in battle (brave old Frank with the empty sleeve) and who, after a brilliant record for headlong valor in the field and an equally brilliant record for exquisite scholarship in the universities at home and in Germany, was struck down by fell disease in the full flush of his young manhood.

Was there ever a nobler, a more inspiring chapter in the educational history of any people? It is a chapter unwritten before, so far as is known to us, and written here only in part. But, such as it is, we hold that it finds a fitting place in the proceedings of this society, whose aim and purpose it is to preserve and transmit to posterity the veracious record of Virginia's glory, not alone in Colonial and Revolutionary times, but down through all the centuries, culminating in those heroic days of 1861-65, when our mother attained what future ages will haply hold the supreme height of her great renown.

PERILS OF STAFF SERVICE.

[During the last two years of the war Maj. Robert R Henry, of Virginia, served on the staffs of Gens. R. H. Anderson and William Mahone. He was three times wounded and had five horses killed under him. The following incidents of thrilling experience in such capacity are taken from a tribute prepared by James P. Whitman, part of which was published as a memorial sketch in the VETERAN for March, 1916, page 126.]

In relating his participation in the battle of Gettysburg, serving on the staff of Gen. R. H. Anderson, Major Henry told of being sent by the General with orders to the division, which at that time was under a severe fire from the enemy's batteries. Before he realized the position in which he was placed, he encountered a sweeping and withering fire of shrapnel and ball so furious and constant that nothing could remain in it alive. After his horse was shot from under him, he threw himself flat on the earth behind a small tree, with his head close to the trunk. The shells having cut the tree almost in two, and fearing it would fall upon and crush him, he arose and fled to a different section of the division, delivered the orders, and returned to the General without receiving a wound—a perilous escape.

The duties of an aid-de-camp on the staff of a fighting general were not those of inaction or sought after by the timid In the latter part of 1864 Gen. G. K. Warren, the Federal commander, had forced back the right wing of Gen. R. E. Lee's army and taken possession of the Weldon Railroad leading from Petersburg; but, unfortunately for Warren, he had not connected his right with the left of the Federal lines and thus left a gap through which Mahone moved his division and attacked Warren's flank and rear. The fighting was severe, and Mahone's Division was about to be cut off and annihilated. Mahone had sent Major Henry to Gen. A. P. Hill for reënforcements, requesting that Gen. Harry Heth's division connect with his lines. But Hill was so hard pressed that he could not comply. After passing through a dense thicket of pines in the execution of this order, Major Henry discovered in a large clearing some distance in his front what seemed to be two batteries of artillery supported by infantry, with a train of ambulances. Seeing that he would be captured if he attempted to cross or flank their line, he turned back to report the situation. He had not gone far when, at a sharp turn in the path a short distance from where he left General Mahone, he suddenly came upon a Federal officer and another mounted man. They were bewildered, evidently lost. Henry drew his Remington revolver and demanded their surrender, which they did without resisting. The pistol was a relic of the Crater and was not in shooting order. He returned to General Mahone with his captives and reported the reason for his failure to find General Hill. Mahone directed him to take the prisoners to division headquarters, from which he returned riding the horse of Col. William Ross Hartshorne, one of the prisoners captured.

In assisting to extricate Mahone's Division from this perilous position, with no hope of reënforcements, Major Henry was severely wounded at Burgess Mill on the 27th of October, 1864, and was unable afterwards to return to duty. General Mahone in his report highly complimented him for his gallant action. Major Henry had a horse shot under him at Gettysburg, another at the Wilderness, one at Spotsylvania, and three around Petersburg, Va., including the one captured from Colonel Hartshorne, two of them being wounded twice.

Coŋfederatҩ Veteraŋ.

57

THE HAMPTON ROADS CONFERENCE.

BY JULIAN S. CARR, DURHAM, N. C.

The True Story of the Hampton Roads Conference between President Lincoln and William H. Seward, on One Side, and Alexander H. Stephens and Other Confederate Commissioners, on the Other Side.

A Refutation of the Statement That Mr. Lincoln Told Alexander Stephens That if He Were Permitted to Write "Union" at the Top the South Might Fill in the Balance.

A Demonstration That Mr. Stephens Never Made Any Such Report.

It is common to hear that President Lincoln at the Hampton Roads Conference during the War between the States said to Vice President Stephens something like this: "Let me write 'Union' at the top of a sheet of paper, and you may write after it whatever you please."

The effect of the story as it is generally told is to make a good impression about President Lincoln and a bad impression about President Davis; the one big-souled and yielding and the other blind and self-destructive.

The beginnings of the story seem to have been very early. The conference was held on February 3, 1865, and on February 6 the Louisville *Democrat* contained this item:

"According to the *Herald's* (New York) correspondent, the President (Lincoln) is reported to have proposed to Messrs. Stephens, Hunter, and Campbell (Confederate commissioners) that if they were prepared to promise the return of their

JULIAN S. CARR,
Past Commander Army of Northern Virginia Department,
U. V. C.

States to the Union he was ready to wave all minor questions but that of Chief Magistrate of the republic, sworn to maintain the Union and laws."

Then in the Augusta (Ga.) *Chronicle and Sentinel* there appeared in the issue of June 7, 1865, what purported to be an interview with Vice President Stephens about the Hampton Roads Conference. (It will be shown later that Mr. Stephens repeatedly and even bitterly complained about the incorrectness and injustice of this article.)

Then Judge John H. Reagan in his "Memoirs" (page 177) mentions the names of four persons who averred that Mr. Stephens himself was the original author of the story—to wit: The Hon. Henry Watterson, of Kentucky; the Rev. E. M Green, of Kentucky; Dr. R. J. Massey, of Georgia; and Mr. Howell, of Georgia. These persons are quoted as saying that they heard Mr. Stephens himself expressly assert it.

In addition to these, Mr. Henry Watterson, in the Louisville *Courier-Journal* of June 20, 1916, avers that Mr. Stephens on the night of his arrival in Richmond from Hampton Roads told this story to "Mr. Felix G. de Fontaine, with whom he lodged and who, when the facts were disputed, made oath to the truth of them." In the same editorial Mr. Watterson says Mr. Stephens said it to him personally.

So the authorship of this story about Union and the sheet of paper is charged to Mr. Alexander H. Stephens, Vice President of the Confederacy and a member of the Hampton Roads Conference.

The purpose of this paper is to examine the available sources of information and follow the data to such a conclusion as the records may warrant. In its preparation the following have been examined and are the basis of its conclusions:

Augusta *Chronicle and Sentinel*, June 7, 1865
Louisville *Democrat*, February 6, 1865.
Louisville *Courier-Journal*, May 2, 1916.
Louisville *Courier-Journal*, June 20, 1916.
Lincoln's "Message to House," February 10, 1865. ("War of the Rebellion," Series I., Volume XLVI., page 505.)
Lincoln's "Instructions to Seward," January 31, 1865 ("War of the Rebellion," Ibid.)
Lincoln's Life," by Nicolay and Hay, Volume X.
Seward's "Letter to Adams." ("War of the Rebellion," Series III., Volume IV., pages 1163-1164.)
"Report of Confederate Commissioners," February 5, 1865. ("War of the Rebellion," Series I., Volume XLVI., page 446.)
Davis's "Message to Congress," February 6, 1865. "War of the Rebellion," Series I, Volume XLVI., page 446.)
Davis's "Rise and Fall of the Confederate Government," Volume II., pages 611-620.
Stephens's "War between the States," Volume II., Chapter XIII. Published 1870.
Stephens's "Pictorial History of the United States."
Stephens's "Recollections," diary kept while a prisoner at Fort Warren; sixteen references to Hampton Roads Conference.
"Stephens's Letters and Speeches," by Henry Cleveland, pages 198-200. Published 1866.
"Stephens's Life," by Pendleton, pages 330-342. Published 1908.
Stephens's five articles in controversy with B. H. Hill in Atlanta *Herald*, April 17, May 8, 25, 31, June 5, 1874.
Campbell's "Recollections." (*Southern Magazine*, December, 1874, page 191.)
Hunter's "Account." ("Southern Historical Society Papers," Volume III., page 175. April, 1877.)

Goode's "Account." "The Forum," Volume XXIX., pages 92-103. March, 1900.)

Hill's "Life, Letters, and Speeches," page 399.

Hill's "Unwritten History of Hampton Roads Conference," Atlanta *Herald* May 3, 1874.

Reagan's "Memoirs," Chapter XIII. Published 1906.

Gordon's "Reminiscences."

Watterson's "Might-Have-Beens of History," *Courier-Journal* May 2 and June 20, 1916.

This conference was held February 3, 1865. Its object was to find, if possible, some terms of ending the war between the Northern and Southern States. It was brought about by Francis P. Blair, Sr., an influential journalist of Washington. He was a native of Abingdon, Va., had lived in Kentucky, but was at this time a citizen of Maryland. He was a Democrat and had been a personal friend of President Davis, but had supported Lincoln for President and fellowshipped with the North during the war.

Blair thought peace might be brought about by getting the two governments to suspend hostilities against each other and join their forces in a common campaign against Maximilian and the French in Mexico in an application of the Monroe Doctrine. He surmised that by the time this task should be finished and because it would be jointly done the animosities between the two sections would be so assuaged that the North and South could settle their differences without further bloodshed. He presented his idea first of all to President Lincoln, who gave him a passport to Richmond. There he laid his project before President Davis in a private interview. Mr. Davis first satisfied himself that he was an informal, though unofficial, representative of President Lincoln, made a written memorandum of the interview, submitted the same to Blair for his approval of its correctness, and on January 12, 1865, gave him a note, in which he said:

"I am willing now, as heretofore, to enter into negotiations for the restoration of peace."

Blair received this note, took it to Washington, and showed it to President Lincoln. He then brought back to Richmond a note dated January 18, 1865, in which Mr. Lincoln said:

"I have constantly been, am now, and shall continue ready to receive any agent whom he or any other influential person now resisting national authority may informally send me with a view of securing peace to the people of our common country."

The way was thus cleared for both Presidents to appoint conferees and arrange for the meeting.

President Davis appointed three commissioners: Vice President Alexander H. Stephens, Senator Robert M. T. Hunter, and Assistant Secretary of War John A. Campbell. He thus intrusted the mission to the gentleman most likely to succeed. All three of them were known to the public as critics of Mr. Davis's administration of Confederate affairs. They persistently believed that the war could be settled by negotiation if only a fair trial were made. They were at least in as good favor at Washington as any men who could be selected, particularly Mr. Stephens. He and Mr. Lincoln had been fellow Whigs and personal friends, and Mr. Lincoln had expressed a desire that he might have him as a member of his Cabinet. He had been opposed to secession from the beginning and had all along been an aggressive advocate of peace by negotiation. The Northern papers of the day were diligently circulating the report that he was on the eve of severing his connection with the Richmond government and the cause of the South. Mr. Hunter was a leading malcontent in the Confederate Senate, and Mr. Lincoln was known to entertain a very high regard for Judge Campbell. Mr. Davis, furthermore, knew that he himself was bitterly disliked at Washington, and this animosity toward him personally would likely handicap any negotiations for peace. He also well understood that if the conference should fail all the blame and censure would be heaped upon him. So he selected conferees who could most likely get favorable terms for the South. He gave his commissioners the following instructions:

"RICHMOND, January 28, 1865.

"In conformity with the letter of Mr. Lincoln, of which the foregoing is a copy, you are to proceed to Washington City for an informal conference with him upon the issues involved in the existing war and for the purpose of securing peace to the two countries.

"With great respect, your obedient servant,

JEFFERSON DAVIS."

He thus left his commissioners untrammeled. The conference they were to go to was to me "informal." The matters they were to confer about were "the issues involved in the existing war." The object which they were to seek was "peace to the two countries." There were no supplementary oral instructions which "tied their hands." Their powers were unqualified except by the terms of the President's written note. There were "two countries" at the moment this note was given, but he did not bind the commissioners to make such a settlement as would leave "two countries" in existence after the conference. The clause about the "two countries" was merely descriptive of the *status quo* at the beginning of the conference.

President Lincoln appointed as his representative his Secretary of State, W. H. Seward, known by every one to be unusually astute, if not foxy, and bitterly hostile to the South. He gave him the following instructions, specifically defining what he was to require as "indispensable":

"EXECUTIVE MANSION, January 31, 1865.

"*Hon. William H. Seward, Secretary of State:* You will proceed to Fortress Monroe, Va., there to meet and informally confer with Messrs. Stephens, Hunter, and Campbell on the basis of my letter to F. P. Blair, Esq., of January 18, 1865, a copy of which you have. You will make known to them that three things are indispensable—to wit: (1) the restoration of the national authority throughout all the States; (2) no receding by the executive of the United States on the slavery question from the position assumed thereon in the late annual message to Congress and in the preceding documents; (3) no cessation of hostilities short of an end of the war and the disbanding of all the forces hostile to the government. You will inform them that all propositions of theirs not inconsistent with the above will be considered and passed upon in a spirit of sincere liberality. You will hear all that they may choose to say and report to me. You will not assume to definitely consummate anything.

"Yours, etc.,   ABRAHAM LINCOLN."

Mr. Seward was thus instructed by his President to require three things as "indispensable" preliminaries to any subsequent terms: (1) Submission, (2) emancipation, (3) disbandment of the Southern armies. Nothing was to be entertained "inconsistent" with these demands.

After many difficulties and much dispatching, the conference was held, not at Washington, but at Hampton Roads on February 3, 1865. When the Confederate commissioners reached the place of meeting, they found that President Lincoln himself had joined Mr. Seward.

The conference was held in the saloon of the River Queen, a small steamer, anchored out in the stream for the sake of greater privacy. The meeting lasted for four hours. It was held behind closed doors. Messrs. Lincoln, Seward, Stephens, Hunter, and Campbell were all present throughout the entire time. Besides these five, no other person entered the room, except that once a negro servant came in and was promptly sent out. At the outset the wily Seward proposed that there be no secretary and nothing like minutes. So no written memorandum of anything said or done was made at the time.

What, then, did transpire at this conference? What terms of peace were offered to the Confederate commissioners? It would seem to be easy to answer this question, because every member of the conference, the only ones who could possibly know, has written and printed and given to the public each his own account of what did occur. And every one of these accounts agree. There is no variation as to the substantive terms that were there proposed. And yet there has been much discussion down to the present day as to what was precisely proposed to the South at that conference. Some contend that the only terms offered were "unconditional submission." Others contend that President Lincoln said to Mr. Stephens, the chairman of the Confederate representatives, words to this effect: "Stephens, let me write 'union,' and you can write after it what you please." And so the great-hearted and generous-minded Lincoln offered them reconciliation and peace on their own terms!

Now let us carefully examine all the available sources of information on this subject and accept the conclusion to which they lead.

PRESIDENT LINCOLN'S ACCOUNT.

The contemporary newspapers of the day filled all the public mind with conjectural reports of what had taken place at Hampton Roads. For example, the Louisville *Democrat* in its issue of February 6, 1865, contained this item:

"According to the *Herald's* correspondent, the President is reported to have proposed to Messrs. Stephens, Hunter, and Campbell that if they were prepared to promise the return of their States to the Union he was ready to waive all minor questions but that of Chief Magistrate of the republic, sworn to maintain the Union and laws."

Then the *Herald* under the same date gives another current report to the effect that "no concession or promise was made by him [Lincoln] in the least degree yielding."

These conflicting newspaper stories led the Federal House of Representatives on February 8 to pass a resolution requesting President Lincoln himself to give a true account of what did happen at Hampton Roads. He complied with this request, and on February 10 sent an official message to the House, purporting to give a correct account of the matter. In this message he first quotes all the letters and telegrams and communications leading up to the conference and then concludes with these words:

"On the morning of the 3d the gentlemen, Messrs. Stephens, Hunter, and Campbell, came aboard our steamer and had an interview with the Secretary of State and myself of several hours' duration. No question of preliminaries to the meeting was then and there made or mentioned. No other person was present. No papers were exchanged or produced, and it was in advance agreed that the conversation was to be informal and verbal merely. On my part the whole substance of the instructions to the Secretary of State, hereinbefore re-

cited, was stated and insisted upon, and nothing was said inconsistent therewith. * * * The conference ended without result. The foregoing, containing, as is believed, all the information sought, is respectfully submitted." ("War of the Rebellion," Series I., Volume XLVI., pages 505-513.)

Mr. Lincoln being the reporter, what did he offer at Hampton Roads? He says, "On my part * * * nothing was said inconsistent" with his instructions to Secretary Seward, and he had instructed Seward to demand three things: (1) Submission to national authority, (2) emancipation of the negroes, (3) disbandment of Confederate armies. But if he said, as is alleged, "Let me write 'union,' and you can write what you please," he said something seriously "inconsistent" with his instructions to Secretary Seward, and his message was not honest and truthful. It is unbelievable that Mr. Lincoln did thus misrepresent the facts to the House. What he himself substantively says he demanded at Hampton Roads was equal to "unconditional submission."

SECRETARY SEWARD'S ACCOUNT.

This is found in a letter to Charles Francis Adams, United States Minister to London. This letter was dated February 7, 1865, four days after the conference, and is printed in the "War of the Rebellion," Series III., Volume IV., pages 1163-1164. In it Mr. Seward says:

"The President 'announced that we can agree to no cessation or suspension of hostilities except on the basis of the disbandment of the insurgent forces and the restoration of national authority throughout all the States in the Union. Collaterally, * * * the President announced that he must not be expected to depart from the positions he had heretofore assumed in his proclamation of emancipation. * * * It was further declared by the President that the complete restoration of the national authority everywhere was an indispensable condition of any assent on our part to whatever form of peace might be proposed.'"

This is not the entire letter, but there is nothing in it which can possibly be construed as inconsistent with what is quoted. Mr. Seward here asserts that the President announced as "indispensable" preconditions: (1) "The disbandment of the insurgent forces," (2) the maintenance of "his proclamation of emancipation," and (3) "the complete restoration of the national authority." All of this means "unconditional submission" and is absolutely inconsistent with anything even approximating, "You can have union on your own terms."

REPORT OF THE CONFEDERATE COMMISSIONERS.

On their return from the Hampton Roads Conference the three Confederate commissioners made a unanimous report of what took place at the meeting. As you read it, as copied below, notice whether there is anything in it that even sounds like Lincoln saying, "Stephens, let me write 'union,' and you can write what you please":

"RICHMOND, VA., February 5, 1865.

"*To the President of the Confederate States—Sir:* Under your letter of appointment of the 28th ult. we proceeded to seek an 'informal conference' with Abraham Lincoln, President of the United States, upon the subject mentioned in the letter. The conference was granted and took place on the 3d inst. on board of a steamer in Hampton Roads, where we met President Lincoln and the Hon. Mr. Seward, Secretary of State of the United States. It continued for several hours and was both full and explicit.

"We learned from them that the message of President Lincoln to the Congress of the United States in December last explains clearly and distinctly his sentiments as to the terms, conditions, and methods of proceeding by which peace can be secured to the people, and we were not informed that they would be modified or altered to obtain that end. We understand from him that no terms or proposals of any treaty or agreement looking to an ultimate settlement would be entertained or made by him with the Confederate States, because that would be a recognition of their existence as a separate power, which under no circumstances would be done, and for this reason that no such terms would be entertained by him from the States separately, that no extended truce or armistice, as at present advised, would be granted without a satisfactory assurance in advance of a complete restoration of the authority of the United States over all places within the States of the Confederacy.

"That whatever consequences may follow from the reëstablishment of that authority must be accepted, but that individuals, subject to pains and penalties under the laws of the United States, might rely upon a very liberal use of the power confided to him to remit those pains and penalties if peace be restored.

"During the conference the proposed amendment to the Constitution of the United States, adopted by Congress on the 31st ult., was brought to our notice. This amendment declares that neither slavery nor involuntary servitude, except for crimes, should exist within the United States or any place within their jurisdiction and that Congress should have power to enforce this amendment by appropriate legislation. Of all the correspondence that preceded the conference herein mentioned and leading to the same you have been informed.

"Very respectfully your obedient servants,
ALEXANDER H. STEPHENS,
ROBERT M. T. HUNTER,
JOHN A. CAMPBELL."

("War of the Rebellion," Series I., Volume XLVI., page 446; Stephens's "War between the States," Volume II., page 792.)

These three signers were competent to tell what transpired at the Hampton Roads Conference, because they were there from its beginning to its end and participated in all its deliberations. Their summing up of the matter was deliberate and was submitted as their official account of what took place. They had every reason to believe that whatever they said would affect the conduct of the President of the Confederacy, of his Congress, of his military department, and react upon the public sentiment of the Southern people. We must believe that their report was serious and that they intended to put Mr. Davis in possession of the exact state of Mr. Lincoln's mind as to the ending of the hostilities between the two sections. We cannot imagine that they were trifling or suppressive or duplicitous. We must hold such gentlemen under such circumstances to have been sincere and honest and fully conscious in this account. Any other view is a grave aspersion upon them.

They formally and officially informed Mr. Davis that Mr. Lincoln would entertain no "terms," or "conditions," or "methods of proceeding," or "proposals," or "agreement," or "truce," or "armistice" "without a satisfactory assurance in advance of a complete restoration of the authority of the United States over all places within the States of the Confederacy." This can mean nothing else under the circumstances but that the Confederate government must first surrender before Mr.

Lincoln would consider Blair's project of applying the Monroe Doctrine to Maximilian and Mexico or anything else. Their report assured Mr. Davis that Mr. Lincoln was implacable and determined to drive the war, without any interruption whatsoever, to utter subjugation. This would not have been true had Mr. Lincoln at any time or in any manner said in words or in substance: "Give me union on your own terms."

Moreover, the three Southern members of this conference were critics and opponents of Mr. Davis's administration. Mr. Stephens was the ringleader of the malcontents and obstructionists at Richmond and soon after this conference left the Confederate Capitol and went to his home in Georgia to nurse his dissatisfaction and disgust with Mr. Davis's conduct of affairs. He and Hunter and Campbell and their like-minded associates were in favor of trying to settle the controversy by some diplomatic compromise, while Mr. Davis felt consistently and persistently persuaded that it would have to be fought to a finish. If, therefore, Mr. Lincoln had said at Hampton Roads, "Let me write 'Union,' and you can write anything else you want," it is inconceivable that these gentlemen, struggling as they had been for some compromise, would not have promptly and avariciously seized upon it, committed the country to it there and then, rushed back to Richmond, proclaimed it, capitalized it, and set to work to put it through. But they did not pursue this course. They came back with the lugubrious report that they found Mr. Lincoln implacable and that he would consider nothing but the complete surrender of the Southern States.

REPORT OF PRESIDENT DAVIS.

The Confederate Commissioners not only made their written report of the conference to President Davis, but Mr. Stephens says: "We reported to him verbally all that had occurred at the conference and much more minutely in detail than I have given you." We may assume that Mr. Davis had full and free interviews with his commissioners after their return to Richmond and that they put him in possession of the minutest inside details of all that was said and done at the meeting. Mr. Stephens says that they withheld nothing, and it is unthinkable that such honorable gentlemen would have kept back one iota of important information. Did they tell Mr. Davis that Mr. Lincoln had said the Confederate government could have union on its own terms?

If they did, Mr. Davis deliberately falsified to the House of Representatives, for on February 6 he sent to that body a formal message in which he said: "The enemy refused. • • • to permit us to have peace on any other basis than our unconditional submission to their rule." ("War of the Rebellion," Series I., Volume XLVI., page 446; Stephens's "War between the States," Volume II., pages 621, 792, 623.) To sustain this interpretation, he laid before the body the written report of the three Confederate commissioners, in which Messrs. Stephens and Hunter and Campbell said: "We understand from him (Lincoln) that no terms or proposals of any treaty or agreement looking to an ultimate settlement would be entertained or made by him with the Confederate States." Messrs. Davis and Stephens and Hunter and Campbell are equally guilty of the grossest misrepresentation and shameful dishonesty if they knew that Mr. Lincoln had said that they could have union on their own terms.

Having sent this account to the House of Representatives, Mr. Davis straightway called for a mass meeting of citizens in the African church, the largest building in Richmond, and made what Mr. Stephens called the most Demosthenian speech since the days of Demosthenes, in which he told his hearers that the Hampton Roads Conference had demonstrated the diplomatic hopelessness of their cause and called upon the country to make a last desperate military effort. Mr. Stephens himself gave up in despair and went to his home in Crawfordsville, Ga. This is all incredible upon the supposition that Mr. Lincoln had said to all the commissioners or to any one of them at Hampton Roads: "You can have union on your own terms."

Did Messrs. Stephens, Hunter, and Campbell consciously misrepresent Mr. Lincoln and impose upon Mr. Davis? They were honorable gentlemen. Did Mr. Davis misrepresent Messrs. Stephens and Hunter and Campbell and impose first upon the Confederate House of Representatives and then upon the public? The thing is unbelievable.

When Mr. Davis sent to the Confederate Congress the report of the Hampton Roads commissioners, the Senate and the House passed joint resolutions. The preamble recited the previous efforts which the government had made to get peace by negotiations and then said concerning the Hampton Roads effort:

"They (the commissioners), 'after a full conference with President Lincoln and Secretary Seward, have reported that they were informed explicitly that the authorities of the United States would hold no negotiations with the Confederate States or any of them separately; that no terms, except such as the conqueror grants to the subjugated, would be extended to the people of these States; and that the subversion of our institutions and a complete submission to their rule was the only condition of peace.'"

Then the Congress passed the resolutions, accepting the issue, calling upon the army and the people to redouble their efforts, and invoking the help of Almighty God. Mr. Stephens was President of the Senate, and Mr. Hunter was a member of it; and we are seriously asked to believe that they sat there and heard this false interpretation of Mr. Lincoln and the conference and saw this desperate action of their Congress without opening their mouths to inform those bodies that they could have union on their own terms. One cannot believe that Mr. Stephens was so guilty.

In reviewing this whole Hampton Roads affair in 1881, when he was writing his great history, Mr. Davis says:

"I think the views of Mr. Lincoln had changed after he wrote the letter to Mr. Blair of June 18, and the change was mainly produced by the report of what he saw and heard at Richmond on the night he (Blair) stayed there." ("Rise and Fall of the Confederate Government," Volume II., page 618.)

It is perfectly certain that Mr. Lincoln had some terms in his mind when he first sent Blair to Mr. Davis. They were probably concessory in their nature. The report somehow got out that he might be in a yielding frame of mind when he should meet the commissioners from the South. Hence the newspapers of the North were circulating it, and when the conference was over the House of Representatives called upon him to report exactly what had been done. Mr. Davis thinks that what he learned from Mr. Blair about the desperate condition of the Confederacy caused him to change his mind. It is also likely that in the interim while the conference was being arranged for he also felt the spirit and temper of those about him who were implacable toward the South. At any rate, Mr. Davis says that the President of the United States declared at the conference that he would accept nothing but "unconditional surrender." We may fairly suppose that

after the lapse of so many years, when writing about it with the war all over, he would have said something about Mr. Lincoln's generous attitude at Hampton Roads if he had ever been told by any of the commissioners that the President of the United States had said to any one of them that the Confederacy could have union on its own terms.

THE STORY OF ALEXANDER H. STEPHENS.

At the time and later a great many divergent reports were spread abroad as to what did actually occur at the Hampton Roads Conference. Mr. Stephens, one of the principal actors in it (and because of these variant reports), devotes the whole of his twenty-third chapter in the second volume of his history of the "War between the States" (published in 1870) to the Hampton Roads Conference. He undertook to give the substance of what each member of the conference said with considerable detail and in the order of each speaker. His chief object was to make public the internal facts of the meeting and clear all misunderstandings and misrepresentations. At the close of his narrative he wrote: "This is as full and accurate an account as I can now give of the origin, the objects, and the conduct of this conference from its beginning to its end." (Page 619.) The following is a fair summary of his long account:

Stephens: "Well, Mr. President, is there no way of putting an end to the present trouble?" (Page 599.)

Lincoln: "There is but one way: those who are resisting the laws of the Union must cease their resistance." (Page 600.)

Campbell: "How can a restoration to the Union take place, assuming that the Confederate States desire it?" (Page 609.)

Lincoln: "By disbanding their armies and permitting the national authorities to resume their functions." (Page 609.)

Hunter: "Then there can be no agreement, no treaty, no stipulation—nothing but unconditional surrender?" (Page 616.)

Seward: "No words like 'unconditional surrender' have been used." (Page 616.)

Hunter: "But you decline to make any agreement with us, and that is tantamount to 'unconditional surrender.'" (Page 617.)

Lincoln: "The executive would exercise the powers of his office with great liberality." (Page 617.)

Stephens: "Mr. President, I hope you will reconsider." (Page 618.)

Lincoln: "Well, Stephens, I will reconsider, but I do not think I will change my mind." (Page 618.)

Boil down this long narrative of Mr. Stephens to a single terse phrase and put that phrase in the mouth of Mr. Lincoln at the conference, and it is not "Union on your terms," but it is "Union on terms of the complete surrender of the South." (Stephens's "War between the States," Volume III., pages 576-624.)

A publication appeared in the Augusta (Ga.) *Chronicle and Sentinel* on June 7, 1865, purporting to give Mr. Stephens's version of the Hampton Roads Conference. It was republished in many other papers. Mr. Stephens in his "Recollections," a diary which he kept while a prisoner in Fort Warren, makes sixteen entries concerning the Hampton Roads Conference, several of them bewailing this newspaper article. He describes it as "a discordant jumble of facts which presents almost anything but the truth" (page 264).

His early biographer, Henry Cleveland, who wrote in 1866, while Mr. Stephens was still alive and accessible, says:

"He (Mr. Stephens) has often been heard to say that his views in consenting to take part in that conference can never be fully understood without a knowledge of the true objects contemplated by the authors of the mission. These he has never disclosed and does not yet feel himself at liberty to disclose. * * * The report (of the commissioners) contains the exact truth touching the points embraced in it; but the real object of that mission was not embraced in it. This was verbally and confidentially communicated." ("Letters and Speeches," pages 198, 199.)

This biographer says that "he (Mr. Stephens) has on several occasions told a few particular friends some things that transpired." Then he adds: "Particularly the agreeableness of the interview, the courteous bearing of Mr. Lincoln and Mr. Seward; but he has always objected to giving the public any account whatever beyond that contained in the official report of the commissioners."

Finally, in 1870 Mr. Stephens told his whole story of the conference in his history and failed to put in it anything like the story of the sheet of paper and union on any terms.

JUDGE CAMPBELL'S ACCOUNT.

This is to be found in the *Southern Magazine* for December, 1874, page 191. This careful, judicious, and judicial gentleman says:

"In conclusion, Mr. Hunter summed up what seemed to be the result of the interview: that there could be no agreements by treaty between the Confederate States and the United States or any agreements between them; that there was nothing left for them but unconditional submission."

According to this member of the commission, they got nothing at Hampton Roads, when all the four hours' conversation was boiled down to its essence, but a proposition of "unconditional submission." This, however, would not be true if Mr. Lincoln said anything approximating, "Let me write 'Union,' and you can write after it what you please."

SENATOR HUNTER'S ACCOUNT.

Both Mr. Stephens in his history and Judge Campbell in his "Recollections" represent Senator Hunter as summing up and reducing to a nut shell the sum and substance of all that had been proposed in the four-hour conference. Consequently great weight ought to be attached to his account of the meeting. It is to be found in the "Southern Historical Society papers," Volume III., pages 168-176. It was written in April, 1877.

Mr. Hunter opens his narrative with some account of the occasion and origin of the conference. Then he says that Mr. Stephens seemed "possessed with the idea that secession was the true remedy for sectional difference," but neither Mr. Lincoln nor Mr. Seward "countenanced the idea for a moment." Then Mr. Stephens "revived the old Monroe Doctrine and suggested that a reunion might be formed on the basis of uniting to drive the French out of America," but Mr. Hunter says: "This was received with even less favor than I expected." Continuing, he says: "Their (Lincoln and Seward) whole object seemed to be to force reunion and an abolition of slavery." Then an "armistice" was proposed and talked about, but it "was promptly opposed by the President and Secretary of State." Then he says: "I asked him (Lincoln) to communicate the terms, if any, upon which he would negotiate with us. He said he could not treat with us with arms in our hands in rebellion, as it were, against the government." Mr. Hunter concludes his story:

"They (Lincoln and Seward) would hint at nothing but unconditional submission, although professing to disclaim any such demand. Reunion and submission seemed their sole conditions. Upon the subject of the forfeiture of lands * * * I said that nothing was left us but absolute submission both as to rights and property. * * * Mr. Seward, it is true, disclaimed all demands for unconditional submission. But what else was the demand for reunion and abolition of slavery without any compensation for the negroes or even absolute safety for property proclaimed to have been forfeited?"

According to this story, at the Hampton Roads Conference the members talked first about "secession" and made no progress toward getting together on that theory. Then they talked about Blair's proposition, the Monroe Doctrine, and Mexico, and still made no progress. Then they conferred about an "armistice," and got nowhere. Then Mr. Hunter asked Mr. Lincoln on what terms they could have reunion, and he would "hint at nothing but unconditional submission." Then Mr. Hunter inquired what safeguards they could expect for their slaves and their property, and Mr. Lincoln referred them to his mercy. Mr. Hunter says (and he was there) "that nothing was left us but absolute submission both as to rights and property." And yet there are some (who were not there) who ask us to believe that Mr. Lincoln said something like this: "You can have union on your own terms."

Mr. Hunter says it was "reunion" that they were talking about, and what the Confederates wanted to know was the terms. Mr. Lincoln "would hint at nothing but unconditional submission." That certainly is not the same thing as saying: "Let me write 'union,' and you can write what you please after it."

CONGRESSMAN GOODE'S ACCOUNT.

Mr. John Goode was a Virginia member of the Confederate Congress in 1865 when the Hampton Roads Conference was held. In the March *Forum* of 1900, Volume XXIX., pages 92-103, he has published his version of this conference. It has an evidential value, because it is based upon a conversation which he had with one of the Confederate commissioners in Richmond soon after his return from Hampton Roads. His story agrees with all the other published accounts. The terms, according to his informant, were "unconditional submission." There is nothing in it which approaches "union and then what you please."

JUDGE REAGAN'S ACCOUNT.

On the formation of the provisional government of the Confederate States at Montgomery, Ala., Mr. John H. Reagan, of Texas, was made Postmaster General in the Cabinet of Mr. Davis and continued in this office to the end of the war. Always in the confidence of his chief and loyal to him throughout the whole conflict, he was taken prisoner with him at the wind-up of it all. He published his "Memoirs" in 1906. He had all the controversies and allegations about the Hampton Roads Conference before him and devoted the thirteenth chapter of his book to the subject. He says:

"During recent years there has been an extensive discussion through the public prints of the questions which arose at the Hampton Roads Conference. It has been asserted over and over that President Lincoln offered to pay $400,000,000 for the slaves of the South to secure an end of the war and that he held up a piece of paper to Mr. Stephens, saying: 'Let me write the word "union" on it, and you may add any other conditions you please if it will give us peace.' I am probably not using the exact words which were employed, but I am expressing the idea given to the public in the discussion. It has frequently been alleged that Mr. Stephens said these offers were made. This has been repeated by citizens of acknowledged ability and high character, and it has been said that these offers could not be acceded to because the instructions given to the commission by President Davis prevented it. * * * I shall submit evidence that no such propositions were ever made."

The "evidence" which Judge Reagan presents is the joint report of the Confederate commissioners to Mr. Davis, the message of Mr. Davis to his Congress based upon that report, the resolutions of the Confederate Congress predicated upon the reports made to them, Mr. Lincoln's message to the Federal House on the subject, and Secretary Seward's letter to Mr. Adams, the American Minister to Great Britain. Then he says:

"While it is true that some respectable men have asserted that Mr. Stephens told them of Mr. Lincoln's alleged offer, * * * and I have all their statements in writing or print, * * * there must have been some misunderstanding as to his language, for he was an honorable and truthful man and a man of too much good sense to have made such allegations in the face of such record as is here presented."

Then Judge Reagan names the following persons as those who have said that Mr. Stephens made the assertions about the piece of paper and union and about the $400,000,000 for the slaves: Hon. Henry Watterson, of Kentucky; Rev. E. A. Green, of Kentucky; Dr. R. J. Massey, of Georgia; and Mr. Howell, of Georgia.

Over against these four he sets the following eight gentlemen who allege that Mr. Stephens denied to them that he ever made such statements: Rev. F. C. Boykin, of Georgia; Mr. R. F. Littig, of Mississippi; Hon. James Orr, of South Carolina; Hon. Frank B. Sexton and Col. Stephen W. Blount, of Texas; Mr. Charles G. Newman, of Arkansas; Gov. A. H. Garland, of Arkansas; and Senator Vest, of Missouri.

Inasmuch as four reputable gentlemen affirm and eight reputable gentlemen deny, Judge Reagan disposes of the matter by saying that "there must have been some misunderstanding as to the language" which Mr. Stephens did use.

COL. HENRY WATTERSON'S ACCOUNT.

Colonel Watterson is the editor of the Louisville *Courier-Journal* and the most brilliant journalist on the American continent. He has recently told the story of the Hampton Roads affair in his newspaper. In an editorial of May 2, 1916, under the caption, "The Might-Have-Beens of History," he says:

"There had been many epistolary and verbal exchanges between the two capitals, Washington and Richmond, before this fateful conference had come to pass. The parties to it were personally well known to each other. Mr. Lincoln and Mr. Stephens were indeed old friends. The proceedings were informal and without ceremony. At the outset it was agreed that no writing or memorandum should be made of what might be said or done. It is known, however, that at a certain point, the President of the United States and the Vice President of the Southern Confederacy sitting a little apart from the rest, Mr. Lincoln took up a sheet of paper and said by way of completing the unreserved conversation that had passed between them: 'Stephens, let me write "union" at the top of this page, and you may write below it whatever you please.' He had already committed himself, in the event that

the Southern armies laid down their arms and the Southern States returned to the Union, to the payment of $400,000,000 for the slaves. That such an opportunity for the South, then on the verge of collapse, to end the war should have been refused will remain forever a mystery bordering on the supernatural."

He then characterizes President Lincoln as "the Christman who had thrown out a life line," wonders if it all were due to "the hand of God," moralizes about Napoleon, and prophesies direfully for the German Kaiser. He then introduces this paragraph:

"It will be recalled that Mr. Jefferson Davis was wont to dwell upon the reluctance with which he quitted the Union and joined in establishing the Confederacy. Yet at the supreme moment he could not see his way clear to an advantageous peace by honorable agreement. He let the golden moment pass and went, taking with him the cause he had maintained during four years so valiantly, to precipitate and complete extinction."

Mr. Davis was not in the conference. We have seen that the report which the commissioners brought back to him informed him "that no terms or proposals of any treaty or agreement looking to an ultimate settlement would be entertained or made by him with the authorities of the Confederate States." If the commissioners told him the truth, that he could get "no terms," how did Mr. Davis "let the golden moment pass"? If Mr. Lincoln said to Mr. Stephens, "Let me write 'union,' and you can write what you please," and Mr. Stephens withheld this information until after the war was over, it would seem that it was he who "let the golden moment pass." Mr. Watterson writes like one obsessed with admiration for Mr. Lincoln, "the Christ-man," and biased against Mr. Davis, the President of the Confederacy.

When his editorial of May 2 was characterized as "fiction" by the Oklahoma City *Times* and the Macon *Telegraph*, Mr. Watterson replied in an editorial of June 20 in the *Courier-Journal*, in which he said:

"That Mr. Lincoln said on the occasion of the Hampton Roads Conference what is denied as 'fiction' rests upon the statement of Mr. Stephens himself made to many persons of the highest credibility. It admits of no doubt whatever. It does not appear in the official documents because it was not a part of the formal proceedings, but an aside during an interview between Mr. Lincoln and Mr. Stephens. They were warm personal friends, old Whig colleagues, Lincoln an ardent admirer of Stephens, whom he wanted to ask to become a member of his Cabinet when he was elected President. The two had drawn apart from the rest. 'Stephens,' said Lincoln, as Mr. Stephens reported the conversation to many of his friends, 'you know I am a fair man, and I know you to be one. Let me write "union" at the top of this page, and you may write below it whatever else you please. I am sure you will write nothing I cannot agree to.' Mr. Stephens replied that the commissioners were limited to treating upon the basis of the recognition of the independence of the Confederacy alone. 'Then, Stephens,' said Lincoln sadly, 'my hands are clean of every drop of blood spilled from this time onward.'"

Mr. Watterson says this story "does not appear in the official documents," and the reason is "because it was no part of the formal proceedings." He has told us that "no writing or memorandum was made," and so there could have been no "official documents" prepared by the conference. He has told us that "the proceedings were informal and without ceremony," and yet he says this story does not "appear" because it is "no part of the formal proceedings." He says it was "an aside," made as a kind of private remark, while Mr. Lincoln and Mr. Stephens were sitting apart from the rest. Continuing in his editorial of June 20, he says:

"Mr. Davis did not see Mr. Stephens at all. But all that Mr. Watterson has averred in this regard was told the night of his arrival in Richmond by Mr. Stephens to Mr. Felix G. DeFontaine, with whom he lodged and who, when the facts were disputed, made oath to the truth of them, as did also Dr. Green, Mr. Stephens's pastor, and Gen. John B. Gordon and Evan P. Howell, of Atlanta, to whom later along Mr. Stephens likewise related them, as indeed he had done to Mr. Watterson himself."

Here Mr. Watterson says, "Mr. Davis did not see Mr. Stephens at all," presumably after his return from Hampton Roads. But Mr. Stephens says in his long narrative in his history: "We reported to him (Davis) verbally all that had occurred at the conference. * * * In this report to him I gave it as my opinion. * * * I called Mr. Davis's attention especially to the fact. * * * I gave it to him as my opinion that there should be no written report by the commissioners touching the conference. * * * I again yielded my views on that point." Mr. Davis did not deal with Mr. Blair in the beginning of this business without making a written memorandum of what was said and submitted it to Mr. Blair. He saw the blunder of the commissioners in making no written memorandum of what was said at Hampton Roads. He wisely required that the report to him should be in black and white, so that he could be protected against misrepresentation in the matter. Mr. Stephens may be believed, and he may be, he did see Mr. Davis after he returned from Hampton Roads and had every opportunity of telling him that Mr. Lincoln had said: "Stephens, let me write 'union' at the top of this page, and you may write below it whatever you please." If Mr. Lincoln said it, why did not Mr. Stephens tell his President, the Confederate Congress, and all the South and change all the results?

Did Mr. Lincoln say it? Did Mr. Stephens say he said it? Here are two questions. Let us take them up separately and see if we are not shut up to Judge Reagan's conclusion that there is a "misunderstanding" somewhere.

1. If Mr. Lincoln said it, his message of February 10 was not frank and disingenuous. It suppressed a vital fact. At that time the newspapers had filled the atmosphere with disturbing reports, some giving it out that the President of the United States had been yielding and others that he had been uncompromising. Besides, there were two groups at Washington vexing Mr. Lincoln, the one urging that terms be made with the South and the other implacable in its attitude and urgings. Here was a context which caused the House of Representatives to ask him for the truth about the matter. He replied, saying he believed his message contained "all the information sought." That message, if our alleged story was fact, ought to have said in substance: "I offered them union on their own terms, and they declined my offer." But his message did not say that. It said: "I offered them the terms I had previously laid down to Secretary Seward—namely, (1) submission, (2) emancipation, (3) disbandment of their armies, and then such mercy as the President of the United States might be pleased to show them." If he thus kept back material fact while professing to give "all the information sought," his admirers must think him something else than "the Christ-man." Had he made such an offer and had

it refused, it is unbelievable that he would not have told the country and extinguished the peace troublers who were tormenting him. Nicolay and Hay, his heroizing biographers, do not put this story into his mouth. Why did they not tell it to illustrate his kindliness and chivalry to his foe? Moreover, why should he have made such a proposition? His game was as good as in his bag, and he knew it. Appomattox was on the 7th of April, and this conference was on the 3d of February preceding.

2. If Mr. Lincoln said it, why did not Messrs. Stephens, Hunter, and Campbell seize upon it, even with avariciousness, and hurry back to Richmond with it and give it out to the President of the Confederacy and to the Southern Congress? They were the leaders of the party at Richmond who desired and believed that peace could be had by negotiation. They had been sent by their Chief Magistrate to the meeting to get the best terms they could, and the terms, according to this story, were, "Union on your own terms." Yet we are asked to believe that they came back and told Mr. Davis and the country that they found Mr. Lincoln implacable—no "terms," "conditions," "proposals," "agreements," "truce," or "armistice" except they "submitted" and threw themselves upon the mercy of the President of the United States. Did they misinform their chief? Did Messrs. Stephens and Hunter sit in Congress the next day and see that body pass resolutions frantically calling upon the country to exert itself to the last extremity because no terms could be had when they privately knew that they could have "union on their own terms"? What right had they to keep back the very heart and substance of what had been proposed at the conference? They were honorable gentlemen. Besides, they were critics of Mr. Davis. Why did they not use the information, if they had it, to triumph over Mr. Davis and save "the golden moment" and the country from "precipitate and complete extinction"? For the sake of a hearsay story lionizing Mr. Lincoln are we to blast the good name of the three Confederate commissioners?

3. If Mr. Lincoln said it only as an "aside" to Mr. Stephens for his private benefit, how was it done? They were all together during the entire time in the cabin of a small steamer. Why should Mr. Lincoln have whispered it to Mr. Stephens so that the others could not hear him? What motive could he have had in such a conference for whispering in the ear of Mr. Stephens, "Any terms you want," and then saying out loud to Messrs Hunter and Campbell, "No terms whatever"? Why should Mr. Stephens receive such an "aside" and keep it from his fellow commissioners? Why did he not get Mr. Lincoln to say it out loud? Why should he keep such a secret from his associates? Carrying such a secret in his bosom, why did he not say to Mr. Davis, "Don't send that message; I have 'aside' information and will seek release from privacy"? Why did he not say to the Congress, "Don't pass those frantic resolutions; I have knowledge up my sleeve"? Secret? Private? Why, Mr. Watterson says he told it to Mr. de Fontaine and Dr. Green the first night he got to Richmond. Why could he not have told Mr. Hunter and Mr. Campbell on the way? If he did, his fellow commissioners were not ignorant of it when they reported to Mr. Davis.

4. If Mr. Lincoln said it to Mr. Stephens as an "aside" and then put him under the bonds of secrecy, why did he not write it down after the war was over and all obligations of secrecy had been removed by the death of Mr. Lincoln and the collapse of the Confederacy? He frequently wrote about the Hampton Roads Conference with the avowed purpose of

telling its whole inside history. Why did he not set down this story in something that he wrote? The public was confused about it. Some were saying that it was true, and some were saying that it was false. He himself became involved in a controversy with Senator B. H. Hill about it. Why did he not put it in black and white? He was a bitter critic of Mr. Davis. In all his voluminous writing about the war after it was all over he ceaselessly put the blame for the failure upon the administration. Upon the supposition that it was fact, can we imagine that he would not have somewhere written it down and upon it made a telling point against the administration? But none can point to the story as put down by his own pen and above his own signature. The best they can do is to try to interpret his written words in such a way as to make them seem to support the story.

5. But they say that Mr. Stephens verbally told this story "to many friends." If eight men, good and true, aver that they heard Mr. Stephens tell this story, eight other men, just as good and just as true, aver that they heard Mr. Stephens say that he did not tell it. If the first eight write or print their assertion, the second eight write or print their assertion. What conclusion shall we reach and rest in? Mr. Stephens was a Christian gentleman of the highest piety, a statesman of the highest honor, a patriot of the purest loyalty. All the records and all the circumstances are inconsistent with the story that he ever said anything like what is imputed to him. He could not have been malignant and vengeful nor yet stupid enough to have withheld from Mr. Davis, his fellow commissioners, the Confederate Congress, and the country at large information which, being known, might have saved "the cause" which Mr. Davis had maintained so "valiantly" for four years from "precipitate and complete extinction."

Judge Reagan's conclusion is the only reasonable and fair one—namely, that there must have been some "misunderstanding" of Mr. Stephens's words when he was speaking freely and conversationally with his friends about the Hampton Roads Conference.

In a recent issue the New York *Times* gave the following account of the Hampton Roads Conference:

"At Hampton Roads he (Lincoln) refused to accept any proposal except unconditional surrender. He promised 'clemency,' but refused to define it, except to say that he individually favored compensation for slave owners and that he would execute the confiscation and other penal acts with the utmost liberality. He made it plain throughout that he was fighting for an idea and that it was useless to talk of compromise until that idea was triumphant. We are aware, of course, of the long-exploded myth telling how he offered Stephens a sheet of paper with 'Union' written on it and told

the Confederate statesman to fill up the rest of the paper to suit himself. 'He offered us nothing but unconditional submission,' said Stephens on his return, and he called the conference therefore 'fruitless and inadequate.'"

The *Courier-Journal* of December 23, 1916, takes this as a text and miswrites again the "long-exploded myth" as veracious history and upon it takes occasion to reflect upon Mr. Davis and to characterize Mr. Lincoln as "a kindly, just man."

How in the name of all that is frank and fair, unbiased, and unprejudiced can the accomplished Southern editor blame Mr. Davis for not taking advantage of information obtained through the Hampton Roads Conference for the benefit of the people over whom he presided? The proposal to hold the conference came to him from Washington; he appointed commissioners out of sympathy with his general administration, honest believers that something could be done by negotiating and more likely to have the favorable ear of Mr. Lincoln than any other persons in the Confederate government; left them, unhampered by instructions, a free hand to do the best they could. These gentlemen brought back the report that they could get no "terms" or "agreements." The conference was a dismal failure because Mr. Lincoln was implacable.

If the Confederate commissioners, all or any one of them, had private and "aside" information that might have been used to the advantage of the Southern people, it was they who suppressed it and voided all the possible results of the conference. No one can believe that Mr. Stephens or Mr. Hunter or Judge Campbell, all or any one of them, were so unpatriotic. This story about "union on your own terms" reflects most upon Mr. Stephens, for the allegation is that it was made known to him privately, and there is no evidence that he ever communicated it to his chief who sent him.

SUMMARY.

The quotations in this brief show that neither President Davis nor Vice President Stephens nor any one of the Confederate commissioners had any public or *sub rosa* information obtained through the Hampton Roads Conference which they failed to make use of to the benefit of the Southern people.

To continue to repeat this story about "union and then what you please," in view of the records presented in this monograph, is nothing short of a fabrication of history. It is based upon reports of the free conversational talks of Mr. Stephens about this meeting, and he was wont to complain with great bitterness about hearsay misrepresentations of him.

All the actors in that celebrated conference are now dead and gone. They were every one gentlemen of the highest reputation and honor. They were all incapable of any unpatriotic or duplicitous action. Each of them, and some of them more than once, has put on record in cold print his account of what transpired at that conference, and neither of them has intimated that there was some vital information that was not revealed or, being known, was not used.

Mr. Lincoln told Congress what he knew about it. Mr. Seward set down in black and white what he knew about it. The three Confederate commissioners, Messrs. Stephens, Hunter, and Campbell, made a formal statement of what they knew about it. These were all the members of the conference and all the persons who could have had first-hand information of what was said and done on February 3, 1865, on board the River Queen at anchor in Hampton Roads. President Davis gave to the Confederate Congress his version of what occurred as it was given to him. Years after the war Mr. Stephens wrote much in books and newspapers about what did occur according to his recollection. Mr. Hunter also set down his recollections, and Judge John A. Campbell also put to record his remembrances of it. Judge John H. Reagan and other gentlemen who were present in Richmond at the time and publicly connected with administrative affairs have also written their versions, gotten from general sources.

In all fairness, these ought to constitute the veracious history of the Hampton Roads Conference, and it is altogether historically illegitimate for any man to read into this record a report founded upon the alleged free conversations of one man, who himself subsequently wrote much on the subject, but nothing which supports the alleged story and which report needlessly reflects upon the honorable participators in that conference.

MISS ADDIE SANDERS.

[From the Memphis Commercial-Appeal.]

When Miss Addie Sanders died at Senatobia, Miss., at the age of seventy-nine years, there passed away a woman whose life was closely interwoven with the best days of the Old South. Born in Denmark, Tenn., she was reared in luxury by an aunt on a beautiful country estate in Virginia. Possessing the advantages of gentle birth and education, she was a belle of ante-bellum days, and during the War between the States her daring spirit led her into adventures which are permitted to few women.

In those years and later there were many suitors for her hand. She enjoyed the society of men. In the drawing-room or in the ballroom she turned a smiling face to chivalry and beauty; but locked in her bosom was the image of "her captain," and to the day of her death she cherished his memory. It was at a popular resort just before the war clouds lowered over the Southland that she met and became engaged to a gallant young Southerner. Then came the call to arms, and he marched away under the Stars and Bars. She never saw him again. His gallantry won promotion for him, and as a captain he laid down his life for his country in the battle of Gettysburg.

In connection with the death of this young officer, Miss Sanders told to a friend the story of an apparition appearing to her on the day a cannon ball ended his life. She was not superstitious, but the visitation was to her so real and so inexplicable that she said to her companion: "John has been killed." Miss Sanders's account of the incident was as follows:

"On horseback Miss Ann —— and I were on our way to collect some money due us for the hire of some slaves. While riding through a lone lane in Panola County, a broad stretch of open country on each side, we heard a horse come galloping through a field, the fallen cornstalks crackling under his feet as he ran. The horse ridden by my companion was spirited, and I told her to jump to the ground for fear the animal would become frightened and run away. Just as she made ready to jump the approaching horse appeared at the roadside, thrust his head over the fence, and neighed—once, twice, three times. The animal was white, bearing cavalry harness and saddle, but riderless. Then as quickly and as mysteriously as he had appeared the horse vanished from sight. My startled companion turned a blanched face to me and said: 'My God, Addie, what does that mean?' To me there was but one answer, and I replied: 'John has been killed.'

"This strange vision, seemingly so real, left its impress on us. To satisfy ourselves, we stopped at the home of my cousin near by and asked him if there were any soldiers in the neighborhood, and when he replied in the negative we related the incident that had just taken place. My cousin then got on his horse and made a search in all directions, but found no trace of the riderless horse. To this day the mystery has not been solved. I should never have mentioned it, so unreasonable it seems, were it not for the fact that my companion was a witness to it.

"A few days later I received a letter notifying me of the death of Captain John, which occurred on the day the riderless white horse appeared to us."

Twice during the war Miss Sanders was held as a prisoner by the Federals, and on one occasion she was mistaken for a Northern spy by the Confederates, but was quickly released with due apologies by the commander for the error. At the time she was on her way from Panola County to a Confederate camp with medicines and clothing for the Southern soldiers. Neither the dangers nor the sorrows of war had altogether subdued her fondness for elegant gowns, and this feminine trait on her part so aroused suspicion that when she reached Hernando she was arrested and taken before Captain Henderson. It required but a few minutes of conversation to convince the captain that a mistake had been made. He informed his men that their beautiful young prisoner was an invaluable aid to his camp, made amends to the fair young captive, and then himself escorted her across the line.

Shortly after the battle of Shiloh, learning that nurses were needed in Memphis, Miss Sanders volunteered her services and labored among the sick and wounded soldiers in the Bluff City. At the time the Ayers Building had been converted into a Confederate hospital.

While accepting the fortunes of war with the best grace possible, it was not to be expected that one so spirited and intensely Southern as she should become reconstructed in a day. She made frequent trips to Memphis by boat. On one occasion she wore a miniature Confederate flag in her hat, and when requested by one of the officers of the boat to remove it she refused. A warm discussion followed. As a last resort the officer threatened to put her off the boat. She boldly stood her ground and defied him. Her persistency won, and she finished the journey unmolested.

Miss Sanders was a devout Christian, a member of the Presbyterian Church, and her genial disposition and unwavering optimism endeared her to a large circle of acquaintances, both old and young.

THE JEFFERSON DAVIS MEMORIAL.

SPEECH OF GEN. BENNETT H. YOUNG AT DALLAS, TEX., NO-
VEMBER 10, 1916, TO THE DAUGHTERS OF THE CONFEDERACY
ON A MEMORIAL TO JEFFERSON DAVIS AT HIS BIRTHPLACE,
FAIRVIEW, KY.

I am much pleased to address an audience on matters which affect the South, its history, its heroism, and its memories, without the possibility of saying aught that will offend any listener. In this large and intelligent constituency, thank God, there is not a single "tenderfoot" when we come to deal with the achievements and record of the Confederate States. Here we can speak candidly, fearlessly, and loyally of the past with only care that we speak truthfully.

The South had an illustrious part in establishing the independence and in creating the glory of this great country of ours. It was a Southern pen, dipped deep in the Southern heart, which drew the immortal Declaration of Independence. It was a Southern military genius who led the toil-worn, battle-scarred, and ragged Colonial patriots to final victory. It was the Southern men from Virginia, Kentucky, North Carolina, and Tennessee who struck the flank of Cornwallis at King's Mountain and sent him limping into the jaws of Washington at Yorktown. And when the Revolutionary War was over and nothing was left but the bill to be paid, the South settled the largest part of that account. Virginia contributed of her domain what is now the States of Kentucky, Ohio, Indiana, Illinois, and Michigan; North Carolina contributed Tennessee; and Georgia donated Alabama and Mississippi. And of the first fifteen Presidents of the new republic, nine of them were from the South and slave-holders. Washington himself being the largest slave-owner on the American continent.

In 1860, when the Northern States, which had been such conspicuous beneficiaries of the Southern States, forced the slavery issue to the point of war, the Southland laid its hand upon Jefferson Davis and charged him with the defense of its rights, its property, and its life. Rich-born, cultured, scholarly, and chivalrous, he was the incarnation of the Southern spirit and the type of the Southern ideal. He belonged to all the South. He was a native of Kentucky; he was adopted by Mississippi; he fought for Texas; he was inaugurated in Alabama; he administered the Confederate government from Virginia; he fled across North and South Carolina; he was captured in Georgia; he lived his patient martyrdom at Beauvoir; he was buried in Louisiana, and his remains now sleep in Virginia, in whose Southern bosom are two other graves, the grave of British sovereignty at Yorktown and the grave of the Father of his Country at Alexandria. Mr. Davis's illustrious character, his splendid patriotism, his lofty ideals, his absolute consecration to duty, his magnificent courage and immeasurable sufferings for the South are each and all a rich heritage which belong equally to all the people of the Confederate States, their descendants, and those who sympathized with the South in its gigantic battling for national independence and national life.

I am here not to beg, but to seek your coöperation in a matter which affects every man and woman in the Southland and to ask your aid in an enterprise which will, if possible, add greater glory to the splendor and renown of Southern womanhood.

When the North had finished its war upon the South, which had so largely created the country, nothing was left to it but name untarnished, honor unsullied, pride unhumbled, and spirit

2***

unbroken. The task which then confronted the Southern people was a double one: First, to retrieve its broken fortunes; and, second, to monumentalize its history and transmit its records to subsequent generations. To achieve the one the sons of the South have wrought valiantly, and to accomplish the other the daughters of the South have labored amazingly and are triumphing gloriously. More monuments to Southern valor have been erected upon Southern soil than have been set up in any other land to any other people.

In this cause of preserving the heroic story of the South and immortalizing its illustrious past the Daughters of the Confederacy have equaled the devotion and loyalty of their mothers, who inspired and suffered throughout the fearful struggle of the sixties. Their task has been to preserve the name and the fame of the land, red with their fathers' blood and drenched with their mothers' tears. The handing down to posterity a correct history of the Southern people and their cause; the casting up of heaps of stone to mark the things that ought to be remembered with pride; the erection of monuments to point their fingers to a sky starred with Southern virtues; the defense of a story that was full of patriotism and glory, of lesson and inspiration—this was the task which the Daughters of the Confederacy laid upon their hearts and to which they stretched out their hands. Who can contemplate the project or behold the triumphant result without placing an amaranthine crown upon the snowy brows of the daughters of Dixie?

I challenge the world to bring out of the annals of the past a story like theirs—of an organization so efficient, of a purpose so lofty, of a resolution so persistent, of a determination so invincible, of a devotion so unselfish, of a spirit so drainless, of a victory so signal. When all the South has brought first a votive offering of frankincense and myrrh and laid it in the lap of those women of the South who lived during the War between the States, it then turns with thankful hands brimful of garlands and flowers, of gratitude and praise and empties them at the feet of the Daughters of the Confederacy and their allied societies. And all the world looks on and applauds the deed and commends the tribute.

At the risk of being considered a retailer of ancient history I may remind you that Jefferson Davis was born one hundred and eight years ago in a little town called Fairview, in Christian County, Ky., halfway between Hopkinsville and Elkton, the county seat of Todd County. When he was eight years old his father removed to Mississippi, and Kentucky lost her son. One hundred and seven years ago Abraham Lincoln was born in Larue County, near Hodgenville, Ky. As the crow flies these two spots are something like one hundred and forty miles apart. Kentucky thus gave in 1861 the two leaders, one President of the United States, the other President of the Confederate States.

Eight years ago Col. S. A. Cunningham, editor of the CONFEDERATE VETERAN, conceived the idea of properly marking the birthplace of Mr. Davis. He prepared a series of resolutions which he submitted to some friends—myself amongst others—and sent them to Glasgow, where the Orphan Brigade was holding one of its annual meetings. At Colonel Cunningham's request General Buckner there presented resolutions suggesting the acquisition, as well as marking, of the birthplace of Mr. Davis. A corporation was organized known as the Jefferson Davis Home Association; of this General Buckner was elected President.

In the course of a few weeks General Buckner sent for me and said: "General Young, I have neither the gifts nor the time nor the strength to make this scheme a success, and I beg of you to do me the kindness to become its President." This I did.

Twenty-one acres of land, covering substantially the birthplace of Mr. Davis, were secured. Options had been taken upon this property, and they were about to expire; the Association had no money and no credit, and I was so fortunate as to be in such a position that I could advance the entire sum necessary to secure the ground, now known as "Jefferson Davis Park." Through these intervening years, through appeals to the men and women of the South, something like $20,000 has been raised, the grounds have been cleared, improved, and on the two street sides inclosed by a handsome stone fence. The State of Kentucky, desiring to do honor to her son, appropriated $7,500 to aid in the work.

With something like $10,000 at our command, we induced Gen. George W. Littlefield, of Texas, to visit the Jefferson Davis Park and look over the work already done and suggest plans for the construction of a suitable memorial to the first and only President of the Confederacy. Sagacious, wise, enthusiastic, successful, and endowed with a large measure of this world's goods, he became deeply interested in the plans for the erection of a memorial that would be worthy of Mr. Davis, as well as worthy of the South, to which Mr. Davis gave more than any man who survived the war. He esteemed it a very high honor to be one of the leaders in this patriotic movement. If carried out along the lines now projected, to him will be justly assigned the chiefest place amongst its promoters.

The women of the South erected at Richmond, where Mr. Davis is buried, a beautiful and imposing monument. The people of New Orleans and their friends have also builded a handsome testimonial indicative of the love the Confederate people had for their President. I can but feel that the world will yet further expect the people of the South in some more extensive and intensive method to show to mankind their appreciation of Mr. Davis's sacrifices and sufferings for his nation. In no other manner can it be done more fittingly than by erecting on the spot where he was born a magnificent, impressive, and distinguishing structure which shall stand through the ages as a silent but eloquent tribute to him who bore in his body and soul dreadful punishment and humiliation because he loved and served his people.

This feeling has been intensified by the fact that recently the United States government has taken over the birthplace of Mr. Lincoln and arranged that it shall be under the care of the American nation, and there are thousands of Confederates and their descendants who will insist that the Daughters of the Confederacy concur in the resolve that something equal in splendor and beauty and grandeur should be erected at the place where Mr. Davis was born. This spirit does not come from the wish to have Mr. Lincoln honored less, but only from the desire to have Mr. Davis honored more. There are a vast number of us who feel that Mr. Davis was a much greater man than Abraham Lincoln and that justice to his talents, justice to his memory, and a protest against the excruciating humiliations which were heaped upon him by his foes all demand with relentless call that the men and women of the South must do as well for Mr. Davis as the nation has done for Mr. Lincoln.

This is a great, my dear auditors, of big things. Little things do not appeal to the human mind in this day and generation. Great things alone can reach the imagination and inspire to the highest and noblest effort.

The chiefest monument builders of the ages were the Egyptians. Their tombs, their mausoleums, their monuments to the dead surpass those of all nations, ancient or modern, and their architects and engineers thought the obelisk the most impressive of all forms of commemorative work. In this country there are four obelisks regarded as the highest in the world. The Washington monument overshadows all other structures of this kind. It is five hundred and fifty-five feet high. It required a government to build it. The Perry column at Put-in-Bay, Ohio, is three hundred and thirty-five feet high. Ohio, Indiana, Michigan, and Kentucky built this. The Bennington monument (at Bennington, Vt.), built to commemorate the great battle at that point during the Revolutionary period, is three hundred feet high. Three States stood behind this memorial. The Bunker Hill monument, for many years the greatest structure of its kind in the world, is two hundred and twenty-one feet high. It was made particularly attractive to Americans because Lafayette in 1825 attended the laying of the corner stone, and the speech of Daniel Webster on that occasion has become the world's classic for similar occasions. The London monument, the best in England, built by Sir Christopher Wren, is only two hundred and two feet high.

After General Littlefield and I had looked over the Davis birthplace, we concluded that we could construct something at Fairview that would be majestic and imposing, not only to this generation, but to all other generations for a thousand years to come, and we thought of an obelisk three hundred and fifty feet high. This would make it the highest creation of a similar nature in the world except the one at Washington. We argued that it was not unreasonable to ask the South and Southern sympathizers to do this great thing. We considered that success would only be possible when we projected it on a scale so large that the structure would strike the beholder with awe by its gigantic proportions and by its immensity create in the human mind profoundest admiration. I do not think anybody will complain because we are seeking in a sense to overshadow the memorial at Mr. Lincoln's birthplace. The South respects the memory of Mr. Lincoln, but the South adores the memory of Jefferson Davis. Mr. Davis was great enough to command the admiration of all men; but when we consider his sufferings and sacrifices for the South, it is his just reward that somewhere in the Confederate States, which he loved so much and where he lived out his days, there shall rise up some structure which, in so far as art in its feebleness can proclaim, shall declare the love and veneration of the people for whom he gave his all—time, money, place, citizenship, health, and lifelong peace.

There are those who believe that Robert E. Lee died of a broken heart. Jefferson Davis survived the war for twenty-five years, but Mr. Davis lived through the sufferings of Fortress Monroe, which have no parallel for their brutality and cruelty in the political history of civilization. He passed with his people through the horrors and persecution of reconstruction. He was denied citizenship, his humanity was cruelly misjudged and slandered. Every possible effort through perjury and false testimony was used to stain his name or to impugn his motives.

Thank God, he was allowed the privilege of witnessing the restoration of all their rights to the seceding States. He looked over his beloved South and saw every political restriction removed and the people restored to their constitutional rights in the republic.

Refused amnesty by the government under whose flag he

VIEW OF THE LANDS OWNED BY THE FATHER OF JEFFERSON DAVIS—FAIRVIEW IN THE DISTANCE.

shed his blood and for whose glory and renown he had offered his life, he calmly and heroically accepted the result which came to him as Chief Executive of the Confederate States. His ambitions were buried in the grave of the Confederacy. The past was a sealed, though a holy, memory. Permitted fourscore years, he let the dead past bury its hopes, and he pointed his people to the future that was full of golden promise. He even prayed for a reunited country. He saw the future as it developed into a complete triumph in all that makes a country great. His beloved Southland grew under the marvelous energies and sagacity of his followers, and her magnificent development won him glory and renown under the leadership of the men who had followed him in the most dreadful war of modern time. The people met bravely the trials and difficulties on every hand. They triumphed wherever truth could prevail, and only great men could win under the tremendous disadvantages they were compelled to face, and their glorious victory in peace brought solace to his spirit, as old age dimmed the forces of his body, but left unimpaired his vigorous mind.

God graciously permitted Jefferson Davis to live a quarter of a century after the cessation of the great struggle, on the Southern side of which he was the controlling spirit. When the end came he looked into the face of death without a quiver. His hands were folded in dignified silence, no word of his stirred ungenerous thoughts or actions in the hearts of his compatriots. He suffered with them and passed through the fires and persecutions of reconstruction which have become, to the minds of all reasonable men, the blackest page in our national history. He emerged from the shameful humiliation of Fortress Monroe with the sympathy and respect of the world, and the clanking of the cruel chains which cowardice and malignity fastened upon his limbs only render his reception of the decrees of fate more beautiful and made him a thousand times more beloved by the people for whom these sufferings and humiliations were endured.

The people of his adopted State would gladly have returned him to the United States Senate, from which he retired to take up the leadership of the Southern people; but he gently yet firmly declined the proffered honor, recognizing that he could serve and help them best by retiring from all public office. He knew that his reappearance in official position would turn loose bitterest venom and fiercest hate, and with manly and philosophical composure he became a looker-on amid the political conflict of that memorable period of the South's history.

The broad mind of Mr. Davis revealed to him that in taking the presidency of the Confederate States he had cast the die for success or failure and that if he failed he would become an alien in his native land. He well understood that failure meant that he would become the most powerless of all who might survive the struggle and that thereafter he could do nothing personally to retrieve the fortunes of those who followed him. He measured up to the highest standard among his associates and companions, and he traveled in no company where he was not the equal of his fellow voyagers.

Aftersight, so much more effective than foresight, in human affairs does not always indicate the correctness of his judgment or the supremacy of his wisdom; * * * but no just man can honestly affirm that any other man of the hour would have made fewer mistakes or proceeded differently with better results. Robert E. Lee, who was in a better position to know all the difficulties Mr. Davis faced, said he believed Mr. Davis did as well as any man could similarly situated, and in the Southland this judgment of Robert E. Lee will remain unchallenged.

Jefferson Davis's courage, loyalty, patriotism, and nobility of soul and heart are enshrined in every Southern mind, and that is a better and grander memorial than any human genius can design. His was a magnificent life, so veracious that no man was ever deceived, so intrepid that no duty was ever shirked, and so pure politically that no flaw has ever been found.

Great as was Mr. Davis, superb as he was in the discharge of all the duties that came into his life as President of the Confederate States, yet, my friends, there was something in the gigantic struggle far greater, far grander than Mr. Davis; it was the spirit and courage that animated the people who constituted the nation of which he was the Chief Executive. While Mr. Davis stands alone by reason of his integrity and his courage and his eloquence, his faithfulness to duty would have made him great under any circumstances with which his life could have been connected. While all this is true, it is also true that Mr. Davis was greatest in his relations to the men and women who shared with him all the burdens that great struggle brought, who faced heroically with him all the vicissitudes of the fateful days from 1861 to 1865, who supported him with a cheerfulness of sacrifice and a unity of patriotism that renders the brief existence of the Confederate nation a story of such marvelous heroism that it touches the highest and noblest sentiments of every honest soul.

No nation or country has ever shown such regard for the memories of its soldiers nor built so many monuments to voice and perpetuate their heroism and their valor. Measured by the length of years and the numbers of survivors, the extent of the monumental construction by the Southern people surpasses all previous annals. These facts demonstrate the power, the persistence, and the indomitable spirit and unconquerable courage of those who constituted the hosts who then stood for what was held by them to be right. There are more monuments to the Confederate cause than have ever been erected to any cause—civil, political, or religious.

The glory of this fact, my friends, is not due to the men who followed the Stars and Bars or wore the gray, but to the invincible spirit of the women of the South. There is no memorial to Jefferson Davis which meets the peculiar conditions which attach to his name. Those which have been erected are artistic and bear upon the imperishable granite of which they are constructed much of love and admiration for Mr. Davis; but however beautiful and indestructible they may be, there is nothing in them just grand enough and great enough for this generation to feel that they justly and truly convey to coming generations the full appreciation of Mr. Davis and his relations to the people of the South. So on the soil of that State where he was born, in the keeping of that commonwealth that gave Jefferson Davis, Albert Sidney Johnston, John C. Breckinridge, John H. Morgan, Roger W. Hanson, Ben Hardin Helm, and forty-two thousand valiant sons to the defense of Confederate rights and the creation of Confederate glory, there ought to be a memorial which will excel and surpass all other monuments built without government aid, it matters not what cause they represent or what name they bear.

A few enthusiastic and earnest spirits have set about to do this great work. I am here to tell you that it shall not fail; that at Fairview there must and will be erected an obelisk which will be amongst the highest and most imposing of such structures in the world outside the Washington Monument. We must see that the men who come afterwards and look upon this magnificent obelisk, towering amongst the clouds, graceful in its lines, superb in its immensity, will thoroughly understand who Jefferson Davis was, what he did, and who were the people that he led and who loved him and made under his guidance transcendent and immeasurable sacrifices for the great principle of self-government.

My friends, I do not think this is an unworthy ambition. I do not think you will say the money and energy which will bring these things about are wasted. In the South we have no great monument of the kind that is proposed to be erected. This one, designed and erected, will be unique in its plan, in its purpose, and in its grandeur.

We come, Daughters of the Confederacy, to ask your co-operation and your assistance. This is a tremendous project, but it is proposed to dedicate this monument within ten months of this date. We want this Association to aid the Jefferson Davis Home Association as one of its chiefest and most prominent workers. We want you to pass a resolution pledging the Association to endeavor to raise amongst its various Chapters and members at least $10,000 to help on with this work. With your unceasing loyalty, your splendid activities, and your unconquerable devotion to all that pertains to the memory of the Confederate States, you cannot very well afford to decline a full and complete part in this great enterprise. It is worthy of you. It is worthy of the Southland. It is worthy of the best men and women the world has ever produced, and we want you to help. I have no doubt at all that when the claims of this work are properly presented to your members not only $10,000 will be raised, but that a greater sum will flow into the Association's treasury from the gentle hands and loving hearts of the Daughters of the Confederacy, who have done more than any other agency in all the world to perpetuate the glories of the heroic story of what the South did and what its people suffered in that great struggle for national life and national independence.

The nation has undertaken the care of the birthplace of Mr. Lincoln in Kentucky. The admirers of Jefferson Davis assure you that his birthplace shall be fittingly cared for. It is understood and believed that Kentucky will do this. As a Kentuckian I declare that the watchful and loving care of that commonwealth that gave more than twelve thousand of its sons to die for the cause of the Southland will see that this park and this monument shall be fully preserved in its beauty, grandeur, and splendor through all the ages to come.

HEARTS OF THE LILIES.

BY GRACE IMOGEN GISH.

We hail in its pride and its beauty
  Our Southland they died to defend;
We love the green meadows spread round us,
  The blue skies that over us bend.
And fair are all blossoms we're bringing
  In memory of soldiers in gray,
But sweetest are hearts of the lilies
  That tell of their glory to-day.

Their war cry is now hushed forever,
  The names that they loved are no more;
No reveille their calm slumber breaking,
  They rest, for their labors are o'er.
Ah! years that are swift in receding,
  Your hallowed scenes slip away,
Like dew on the hearts of the lilies
  That tell of their glory to-day.

And so when, the blue sky above us,
  Together united we stand
And list to the sweet strains of "Dixie,"
  We think of that lessening band;
We think of the comrades that await them,
  The joy at the end of life's way,
As bright as the hearts of the lilies
  That tell of their glory to-day.

O hills, lift your heads in the sunlight!
  O valleys, grow wondrously fair!
O mountains, be steadfast as they were
  Who guarded our land with such care!
O rivers, sing ever their praises
  Till we, of good courage as they,
May grow pure in heart like the lilies
  That tell of their glory to-day!

THE BATTLE OF SHILOH.

BY JASPER KELSEY, SECOND LIEUTENANT COMPANY A,
23D TENNESSEE REGIMENT.

At one o'clock on the morning of April 3, 1862, the Army of the Mississippi, which had been concentrated at and around Corinth, Miss., in command of Gen. Albert Sidney Johnston, with Gen. G. T. Beauregard second in command, was ordered to be ready to march at any moment with five days' rations and one hundred rounds of ammunition. It was also understood by many officers, and even by many private soldiers, that a great battle was to be fought; and every man was full of patriotism and enthusiasm, ready for the conflict. We had lost Fort Donelson, Bowling Green, Southern Kentucky, and Middle Tennessee, and this army had not as yet gained a decided victory in battle, and a greater part of the men had never been in a battle. The army was well organized, well drilled, and well seasoned, considering the length of time it had been in service, which was from a few months to about a year. While all had a sufficient supply of rations and clothing, not all were well armed. Several thousand Enfield rifles with accouterments were issued about that time. We received orders from General Johnston to aim low, to shoot at the knees, because it took about two men to carry one wounded man off the field; but a dead man needed no attention, so it would weaken the enemy more to wound a man than to kill him. An order was issued that no soldier should leave the ranks to attend to a wounded comrade, but to let the infirmary corps attend to them; also an order was given that when any soldier or company got lost from their command in time of the battle they should go where the heaviest firing was, because the battle ground was covered with forests, hills, ravines, and swamps. On the evening of the 3d the army was put in motion, marching in the direction of Pittsburg Landing, on the west bank of the Tennessee River and about twenty-two miles from Corinth, where the Federal army was encamped under the command of Generals Grant and Sherman and about 49,314 strong.

The Confederate army consisted of three army corps, the first commanded by General Polk, the second by General Bragg, and the third by General Hardee—about 35,000 or 36,000 men exclusive of the cavalry, which numbered 4,300 and which could do but little service except to guard the flanks, owing to the nature of the ground on which the battle was fought. General Hardee was ordered to form the first line of battle with his corps in front of the Federals. General Bragg was to form the second line with his corps about eight hundred yards in the rear of Hardee's Corps, and General Polk was to put his corps in line, or in double column, in the rear of Bragg's line. General Breckinridge's command was to be placed on the right of Polk's Corps as a reserve, while the cavalry was to be placed on the flanks and in position to guard the fords of Lick Creek on the right and Owl Creek on the left.

We met with no resistance from the enemy from the time of leaving Corinth until reaching the ground where the lines were to be formed except that on the 4th Cleburne's Brigade, of Hardee's Corps, met and repulsed a small detachment of the enemy's cavalry. On Friday there were cold, drenching rains which made it very disagreeable for the soldiers, and roads in some places were almost impassable. By nine o'clock on Saturday the clouds had passed away, and there was fine spring weather until the battle was over.

On the morning of the 5th General Hardee reached the place designated and deployed his corps in line of battle on the high ground between Owl Creek on the north and Lick Creek on the south, with the left wing near Owl Creek and the right near Lick. The creeks were about three miles apart, running in a northeastern direction and emptying into the Tennessee River, one above and the other below Pittsburg Landing, so that the line of battle was about three miles in length and about two miles from the Federal encampment. General Johnston intended to attack the Federals on Saturday morning, but on account of the heavy rains and bad roads and some misunderstanding a portion of Bragg's and Polk's Corps did not arrive and deploy in line before about four o'clock Saturday in the afternoon; so it was too late to make the attack on that day as intended. Late Saturday evening Johnston, Beauregard, Bragg, Polk, Breckinridge, and perhaps some other officers met in a consultation. Beauregard was opposed to giving battle and favored withdrawing and marching back to Corinth. His reasons were that one day had been lost, that he believed the Federals were strongly fortified, and that they had a much larger army than the Confederates.

General Johnston said he had as many men as he could manage on the ground between the two creeks, and he knew he could handle as many as the enemy, his flanks being protected by the two creeks, and, said he, "We will fight them if there are a million of them"; and he gave orders for the battle to begin at daylight Sunday morning, April 6. Here was assembled an army of brave men, the flower of the South, mostly from Tennessee, Kentucky, Louisiana, Mississippi, and Arkansas, commanded by one of the greatest generals on the American continent, who had served in the Black Hawk War, in the Texas War of Independence, the Mexican War, and in command of the United States army that subdued the Mormon rebellion—Gen. Albert Sidney Johnston.

The army silently and quietly bivouacked in line of battle for the night, while in the Federal encampment, about two miles in front of the Confederate lines, music and cheering could be heard until midnight. They were serenading some officers' headquarters, not knowing of the nearness of the Confederate army or dreaming of the fierce conflict that was to take place on the morrow. On Sunday morning before daylight the oak forest was alive with Confederate soldiers eating their cold breakfast, preparing their weapons, and falling into line to be ready for the great battle which every man knew was going to take place. At daylight Hardee's line, three miles in length, without the sound of bugle or drum, advanced silently and grandly against the Federal encampment, followed by the sturdy solid lines of Bragg, Polk, and Breckinridge. The morning was bright and clear, a typical spring morning; the air was fresh and bracing; and when the sun rose bright and clear it added splendor to the scene. Every soldier had braced himself for the battle and went forward determined to reclaim the ground recently lost or die in the attempt. Gen. Basil Duke says in his "History of Morgan's Cavalry": "Every one who witnessed the scene—the marshaling of the Confederate army for the attack on the morning of the 6th of April—must remember more distinctly than anything else the glowing enthusiasm of the men, their buoyancy and spirited impatience to close with the enemy."

At 5:14 Hardee's line came in contact with the Federal outpost, and the first gun of Shiloh was fired; then began one of the hardest-fought battles of the war. The Confederate lines moved quickly and steadily forward. The Rebel yell was heard mingled with the rattle of muskets, the roar of cannons, and the bursting of shells. Soldiers were falling, dead or wounded, upon the right and the left. That was a time to test the bravery of men. Quoted from Beauregard's report: "Like an Alpine avalanche, our troops moved forward, despite the determined resistance of the enemy, until 6 P.M., when we were in possession of all his encampments between Owl and Lick Creeks but one, nearly all his field artillery, about thirty flags, colors, and standards, over three thousand prisoners, including a division commander (General Prentiss) and several brigade commanders, thousands of small arms, an immense supply of subsistence, forage, and munitions of war, and a large amount of means of transportation—all the substantial fruits of a complete victory. The remnant of his army had been driven in utter disorder to the immediate vicinity of Pittsburg Landing under the shelter of the heavy guns of his ironclad gunboats."

It happened that, though the first collision between the two armies was with Prentiss's outposts, it occurred nearer to Sherman's camp than to his own; and as his lines were more retired than Sherman's, the first blow fell upon the left brigade of the latter under Hildebrand. This lay in the pathway of the impetuous Hindman, and the swiftest of the fugitives, scattering through the Federal camps, gave the alarm; the rattle of musketry also gave sharper notice that it was no common peril that threatened. The long roll was beaten, the bugle sounded, and brisk volleys gave still sterner warning. and Sherman's division woke to find the Confederates pressing right upon them. Sherman hurriedly formed his line of battle in front of the camp. It was good ground for defense—a low timbered ridge, with an open valley, traversed by a small stream, in front. To attack them the Southern brigades had to cross the stream and open field. The Confederate line, which had hung for a few minutes only on the crest of the hill, like a storm cloud on the mountain's brow now burst with a sudden impulse upon Sherman's camps. The Rebel yell, so inspiring to friends, so terrific to foes, rose sharp and shrill from the rushing lines of Southern soldiers; their volley came pouring in, and the bayonet even was used on some whose slumbers were broken only by the oncoming of their foes.

Sherman's orderly was shot dead by his side, and he himself rode away to the right out of the wreck. Then Hildebrand's Brigade, of Sherman's Division, was beaten and fled from the field in wild disorder. While this struggle was going on Hindman's right brigade, under Colonel Shaver, and Gladden's Brigade burst in upon Prentiss's Division. It was not eight o'clock when Shaver's and Gladden's strong lines fell fiercely upon them. Here was enacted, though in a less measure, the same scenes that had occurred in Hildebrand's camps. Crowded in front, to the right, to the left by eager antagonists, Prentiss's whole division gave way and fell back in confusion on its supports. At the first alarm Sherman sent back to McClernand, Hurlbut, and W. H. L. Wallace for help. McClernand hurried three Illinois regiments to the front, which, arriving just as Hildebrand was routed, were unable long to withstand the vigorous attack of Hindman's brigades as they pushed on in their victorious career, part of Shaver's Brigade, coming to Wood's assistance, breaking in on the left flank of the Illinois regiment. Assailed, beset, shivered, these gallant Northwestern troops gave way. In their demolition Waterhouse's Battery fell into the hands of Wood's Brigade. It was charged and taken by the 16th Alabama and 27th Tennessee Regiments. When Hardee's first line of battle was formed, Chalmers's Brigade occupied the right flank near

Lick Creek, Cleburne on the extreme left leading his brigade against Sherman's right.

Sherman's strong position has already been described. The ravine that fronted it descended rapidly to Owl Creek, spreading into a marsh filled with undergrowth and tangled vines. The assailants had to cross this under fire and charge up a steep acclivity, though more to the right the ground was less difficult. The center of the morass was impassable and split the brigade into two parts. The 5th, 24th, and 2d Tennessee passing to the left, the 23d Tennessee was divided, the left wing going to the left, the right wing, with the 6th Mississippi, passing to the right. The 15th Arkansas, which was deployed as skirmishers, fell back on its supports. Never was there a more gallant attack or a more stubborn resistance. Under the terrible fire from Sherman's impregnable lines the 23d Tennessee on reaching the swamp wavered and fell back about fifty or seventy-five yards, then went forward, and the right wing charged immediately into the Federal encampment; the left wing followed, and the regiment re-formed in line of battle and continued in pursuit of the retreating Federals. Then Lieutenant Colonel Neill, commanding the 23d Tennessee, was severely wounded, Major Moore was killed, and Captain Harden was severely wounded.

The 6th Mississippi suffered a quick and bloody repulse, losing, after making charge after charge, its two field officers, Colonel Thornton and Major Lowry, both wounded, and three hundred men killed and wounded out of four hundred and twenty-five. The fighting had been murderous on the left also. The 15th Arkansas had lost its major, J. T. Harris, and many good men. The 24th Tennessee had borne itself with steady valor, and the 2d Tennessee, commanded by Col. (afterwards Gen.) William B. Bate, had been terribly cut up by the iron storm from the hilltop. This regiment was on the extreme left, and it is said that the fire there encountered was the worst the regiment suffered during the war except at Richmond, Ky. The regiment was repulsed with the loss of Maj. W. R. Doak, Captains Tyree and Bate, and two lieutenants killed, and nearly a hundred men and officers killed and wounded out of three hundred and sixty-five men on the field. But the regiment re-formed, and the gallant Bate led them again to the charge. As he was crossing the creek at the bottom of the valley a Minie ball crushed his leg bone and wounded his horse. He pressed on until he was too weak, when he retired. The 24th Tennessee, being on more favorable ground. clung to the advanced position it had won. It too suffered heavily, losing over two hundred in killed and wounded.

Sherman's position was the strongest point on the line and virtually impregnable to a direct attack. At this time two brigades of Bragg's Corps, which had now come up, attacked Sherman's left and rendered his position no longer tenable, and his brigades fell back, fighting confusedly, on Hurlbut's and Wallace's line. Captain Behr was shot from his horse and his battery taken at the point of the bayonet, his men barely escaping. Another battery, commanded by Lieutenant Colonel Strahl, was charged and captured by the 4th Tennessee, the regiment losing in the charge thirty-one men killed and one hundred and sixty wounded. In the meantime Russell's Brigade charged a battery and helped to drive the enemy some five hundred yards. This was part of a simultaneous advance which drove Sherman from his first position and in which Cleburne's, B. R. Johnson's, and Stewart's brigades joined. Johnson himself was finally wounded. Preston Smith then took command of the brigade; his regiment and Blythe's Mississippi had already captured six guns. The whole Federal front had been broken here and there, and they fell back across a ravine to another strong position; but they were not allowed to get away unnoticed. They were pursued, driven and slaughtered as they fell back, and the route of his retreat was marked by the thick-strewn corpses of his soldiers. Sherman was not allowed to remain in his new position; Polk attacked him with two brigades. The Federals fought with determined courage, contesting every inch of ground. Here Brigadier General Clark and B. R. Johnson were severely wounded, and Colonel Blythe, of Mississippi, was killed. The loss was severe, but the enemy was dislodged and two batteries captured. There the right wing of the Confederate lines was swung around on the center, Hindman's Brigade as a pivot, so that every command of the Federals was taken successively in front and flank, and a crumbling process ensued by which the whole line went to pieces.

General Chalmers, on the extreme right, swept down the left bank of Lick Creek, driving in the pickets, until they encountered the brigades of Stewart and McArthur. Stewart was strongly posted on a steep hill near the river covered with thick undergrowth and with an open field in front. McArthur was to his right and near the woods. Jackson attacked McArthur, who fell back, and Chalmers went at Stewart's Brigade. This command reserved its fire until Chalmers's men were within forty yards and then delivered a heavy and destructive volley, but after a hard fight they were driven back down the river. Chalmers's right now rested on the Tennessee River bottom lands, and he fought down the bank toward Pittsburg Landing. The Federal left was completely turned and their army crowded on a shorter line, a mile or more to the rear of its first position. This was all done and the Federals had established their new lines before ten o'clock. Thus far all had been successful. The second line of the Federals was shorter and more compact than the first, with its right resting on Owl Creek and its left near the bank of the Tennessee River.

The whole Confederate army had become engaged in the battle and was in the front line, Breckinridge on the right, Polk and Bragg in the center, and Hardee on the left. The advance of the Confederates had been steady up to about 1 P.M., when the right wing encountered such resistance as prevented its farther advance. The Confederates were upon a ridge, while upon a parallel ridge in easy musket range the Federals were in great force. After the fire had been continued about an hour, General Johnston ordered a charge, and he and General Breckinridge led in the charge. Governor Harris also led a Tennessee regiment in this bloody charge. The line moved forward with rapid and resistless step. A sheet of flame burst from the Federal stronghold and blazed along the crest of the ridge. There was a roar of cannon and musketry, a storm of lead and iron, and the Confederate line withered, and its dead and dying strewed the dark valley; but there was not an instant's pause. Right up the steep they went. The crest was gained, and the enemy was in flight, a few scattering shots replying to the ringing yell of the victorious Confederates.

A short time after this charge was made it was seen that General Johnston was wounded. Governor Harris and Captain Wickham helped him from his horse, and he was dead in a few minutes. Just when General Johnston was killed the victory seemed complete. The enemy was not merely broken, but was in such close quarters and so rapid was the charge that they suffered more than the usual slaughter in a defeat. Then there came a lull in the conflict on the right, lasting

more than an hour from half past two, the time at which General Johnston fell. About 3:30 the struggle at the center was renewed with the utmost fury. Polk's and Bragg's Corps, intermingled, were engaged in a death grapple with the sturdy commands of Wallace and Prentiss. The Federals had consulted and resolved to stand and hold the ground at all hazards, hoping thus to save the rest of the army from destruction. This manful resistance cost one his life and one his liberty. They checked the Confederates enough to gain some time and perhaps prevented the capture of Grant's army. General Ruggles collected all the artillery he could find, some eleven batteries in all, which he massed against Prentiss's right flank. The opening of so heavy a fire and the simultaneous advance of the whole Confederate line resulted at first in the confusion of the enemy and then in the defeat of Wallace and the surrender of Prentiss.

But while the artillery massed by Ruggles and his division was so effective in achieving this result, they were not alone. Polk and Hardee burst through and destroyed the troops occupying the right of Wallace's position, who were thoroughly beaten and driven from the field or captured and their commander killed in the riot. They thus got in on Prentiss's right flank. Bragg, who had gone to the Confederate right with Breckinridge, pushed in on Prentiss's left flank and, with Chalmers on his rear, thus intercepted his retreat. Immediately after the surrender of Prentiss General Polk ordered a detachment of cavalry to charge the fleeing enemy, which dashed forward and intercepted a battery, the 2d Michigan, within one hundred and fifty yards of the river and captured it before it could unlimber and fire. It was a six-gun battery and was captured, men, horses, and guns.

This was about the end of the battle for that day. It is true that there was some more fighting and advancing of the Confederate lines; but General Beauregard sent orders to the troops to retire and rest for the night, which they did, except Chalmers, who kept up the battle with his command until night, not having received the orders of Beauregard to retire.

Thus ended the first day of the battle of Shiloh. The Confederates slept in the tents which had been occupied by the Federals on the night before, while the Federals were reforming their lines and Buell was crossing his troops over the river and making preparations for the battle which was to begin on the next morning. On Monday morning Grant had about twenty thousand effective men. Buell had come up and crossed the Tennessee River with about twenty thousand, making the Federal army number about forty-five thousand men. General Beauregard, who took command of the Confederate army after the death of General Johnston, had about twenty thousand effective men on the field with which to meet the overwhelming forces of the enemy. The Confederates, though almost worn out by the hard fighting of the day before, marched out, formed in line of battle, met the enemy, and fought bravely for some time, but could not long hold their own against such overwhelming forces. Soon the line became thin, wavered, and began to give ground, fighting bravely as they retired. There was hard fighting all along the line, some of the Confederate commands holding their positions or falling back slowly, taking new positions and fighting fiercely until by one o'clock it was apparent to General Beauregard that the contest was hopeless. The movement of the Federal army was that of the tide as it crawls up the beach. Each living ripple was rolled back at the musket's mouth, and yet, after seven hours' struggle, the Confederates had lost ground and were evidently maintaining a hopeless conflict. There was no reason for remaining there without a chance of victory. Beauregard at last determined to retreat and made his disposition judiciously to that end. In a lull of temporary success he retired his right wing in good order. The retreat was by alternate lines and was skillfully conducted. About an hour after the Confederate troops retired the Federal army reoccupied its front lines of April 5. The only attempt of the Federals to follow up the victory was on Tuesday. A force of Federal infantry and cavalry attacked the Confederate rear guard, which was commanded by Colonel Forrest, and was repulsed with considerable loss.

Thus ended the battle of Shiloh, one of the hardest-fought and bloodiest of the war—the one great army contending for State rights, self-government, and because their country was invaded; the other for the Union and centralizing government; both for what they conceived to be their rights. The Confederates learned in that battle that one Southern man could not whip ten Yankees, and the Yankees learned that it was necessary to carry the spade with them as well as the gun.

(Although a participant in the battle, the author of this paper is indebted for many of the above facts to Col. William P. Johnston's "Life of Gen. Albert Sidney Johnston.")

CHICKAMAUGA AS I SAW IT.

BY ELDER J. K. WOMACK, PLANT CITY, FLA.

It was Sunday, September 20, 1863. After forming and reforming Baxter Smith's regiment, Paul Anderson commanding (it was known as "Paul's People"), the men were numbered off, "One, two, three, four, five." The trooper who was numbered five shouted very distinctly "Bully." Paul said very clearly through his nose: "Let 'Bully' go into the fight and number four hold horses."

Skirmishes being on some distance in front, I remember seeing Captain Lester, of Lebanon, Tenn., who was by far the best-looking man in the regiment, as we slowly marched toward the enemy. The command "Charge!" came in distinct tones. All went forward with a rush. I could still see the long black hair of Captain Lester, which seemed to quiver from the Minie balls that filled the air around us.

Before this charge was ordered, in marching slowly through the woods, where bomb shells were heard shrieking, Colonel Anderson would cry out: "Lie down, boys!" Flat to the earth we stuck like lizards. When the bombs passed over us and burst, "Up and forward!" and again, "Lie down, boys!" we heard, and quickly we obeyed, becoming lizards again by hugging the earth. In a few seconds a bomb in some mysterious way exploded only a few feet over our heads. Without orders from colonel or captain, we struck the earth with a thud.

"Ha! ha! ha!" was heard from the colonel. "Too late now, boys." Turning my head a little to the left, I saw Colonel Anderson standing, tall and erect, laughing at our predicament. I noticed that he remained erect all the time, so I thought in my boyish mind: "If you don't lie down, neither will I. Do you think that we are cowards and you the only brave man in this regiment? I will not lie down any more if you stand upright."

So the laugh from our colonel drove all the fear from me during the whole day. I shall never forget how the enemy, concealed behind trees and logs, poured a volley of leaden hail into us. Captain Parton, of East Tennessee, fell near me with his left thigh crushed. Cartridge boxes were shot off; men were wounded right and left. The enemy was driven before us with a rush. Orders came to "Halt! Fall back to your horses and mount them!" As I walked along to the horses in the rear I saw dead Confederate soldiers and then dead Yankees. In a few steps I came to a wounded Federal soldier whose face I liked as soon as I saw him. "What can I do for you," said I. "Nothing," was the reply, "for I think I will soon be dead." Upon getting closer I saw he had only a flesh wound and had not bled much. "Friend, you are not hurt much, and you can get well if you will try. You are just sick from the wound."

One of my own company (M—) cried out from a distance: "I am going to take his boots." I had noticed they were extra fine, to my mind worth about twelve dollars. "No," said I; "you cannot take his boots. This is my prisoner, and I will see that his boots are not taken from him." Upon coming closer M— swore that he would take the boots; so I tried to reason with him, but without effect, as he continued to clamor for the boots. At last I said: "This is my prisoner, and as long as I have a load in my gun you are not going to take them." The wounded Yankee had not at first looked at me, but he now turned his head and was looking me squarely in the face. I shall never forget the kind expression and evidence of confidence he had in me. I said to my comrade: "I would go barefooted the rest of my days before I would take the boots off of a wounded man." As the man wished to be moved to the shade of a tree, I ordered M— to help me, and we placed him in the shade. I put a soft chunk under his head, took off his boots, and placed them under his head on the chunk, as the tops of the boots were soft and made a good pillow. I then bade him good-by, expressing the hope that he would get back to his people.

I was immediately detailed to go to the rear to wait on the wounded of our brigade. This was two or three miles to th rear, and when I got there I found that the hospital was an old log house, the floor covered with the wounded of our brigade. A small space in the middle was left so the nurses could walk between the wounded. Here I found Captain Parton, whom I saw fall in battle. One or two were almost crazy from wounds. I noticed one trooper take his pistol from the scabbard and point forward, saying: "I am going to shoot the Yankees." Having only two nurses to twenty-five or thirty men, we quietly slipped the pistols from all we could and hid them in the corner of the house.

About eight days later I was called back to my regiment. In passing back over the battle field I saw wounded and dead Federals lying in a space not larger than twenty-five feet square who had never been touched by nurse or doctor. They were crying, "Water, water, water," their long hair standing out in all directions, glued together with blood. The dead among them were swollen twice or three times their natural size. But I noticed no dead or wounded Confederates. I was anxious to know why the Federals had not looked after their men; but when I passed by a very large tent flying the United States flag, I saw wounded Federals lying as thick as they could be placed.

And this was war, and "war is hell." O that we could have had a Woodrow Wilson at Washington then as now!

THAT FURLOUGH.

BY R. J. DEW, TRENTON, TENN.

During the winter of 1864, while the Army of Tennessee was camped at Dalton, Ga., I asked for a furlough to Oxford, Miss., as Tennessee was at that time held by the enemy. To my surprise, my request was granted; so early in the morning Lieutenant Day (now Rev. J. B. Day) and I bade farewell to the boys with hearts set on going to West Tennessee. The evening of the first day found us in Atlanta, and after a short stay we were soon on the road to Montgomery; but before reaching that city we heard bad news regarding our trip, and Lieutenant Day, deciding to take no risks, spent his time with the good people of Opelika. However, I went on, feeling lonely over the loss of my traveling companion. On reaching Montgomery I learned that I could not get a boat until the next evening. Late in that afternoon the hoarse whistle warned me that she would soon weigh anchor. Haversack in hand, I hurried toward the river, but imagine my surprise before reaching the wharf to see Lieutenant Day standing on the hurricane roof waving his hat. Feeling blue over being left, he had taken the next train and was first on board the boat. It was a happy meeting. A pleasant trip down the Alabama brought us the next day to Selma, only to meet additional discouragement. Furloughed soldiers returning to camp told us that we could not pass Demopolis. We were greatly upset, but took the first train in that direction. On the way we held a counsel as to farther plans. Day decided that the trip would be too hazardous, but I was still determined to go on. The train slowed up and stopped on a big farm, and on leaving the car Day said, "I will spend my furlough at the farmhouse yonder," at the same time handing me a letter to his wife. With a warm grasp of the hand, he was off. The train moved on; our journey together had ended.

Just as the train moved off a soldier boy, a mere youth, slender and pale, who had heard our conversation, came and asked that he might go along with me to his home in Tennessee. I surveyed the little stranger closely, at last telling him regretfully that when I left the railroad, which I expected to do soon, he could never keep up with me; that I belonged to the infantry. He insisted, as only a boy can, that he could and would give me no trouble. His youthful appearance touched my sympathy, and when I consented to take him the joy of his countenance repaid me. We left the railroad before reaching Demopolis and took up line of march northwest, meeting before we reached Columbus, Miss., many families refugeeing, almost panic-stricken, before the reported advance of General Smith, who was at the time moving south from Memphis. The constant warning of these people caused us to change our route; so we turned north into the mountains of Alabama, keeping the Tombigbee between us and the Yankees and walking almost around the headwaters of that river through a country at that time dangerous. After encountering many sad disappointments, we at length reached Iuka, Miss., with only one word of cheer, that from Major McNairy, of General Cheatham's staff, whom by chance we met.

Leaving Iuka the next evening, we found ourselves in a deserted waste of country on the banks of the Tennessee, night approaching and lost, badly lost. The Yankees tented on the other side of the river. Bewildered, we stood gazing, and while thus engaged two or three soldiers got into a big skiff, taking a dog with them, and began to row toward us.

That made me nervous. I turned to the boy and said: "They will try to capture us with the dog. We must get away so we can kill the dog before the soldiers overtake us." With this warning, like a deer I went through the woods, closely followed by my little comrade, not stopping until we were lost in darkness. We heard nothing more of the soldiers or their dog. After hours of wandering in the dark the rest of the night was spent on Shiloh battle field with some kind old people. We occupied an office room in their yard. Worn out with fatigue, the boy was sleeping sweetly when at early dawn our host crept softly in and made us a fire. While sitting there, patiently awaiting our awakening, in walked two savage-looking men with murderous old rifles. After some minor questions they asked about us. In bed and without the shadow of a chance to escape, I thought my time had come. But the old gentleman, used to emergencies, assured them that we were Rebel deserters going home, at which they seemed satisfied and soon left. Our host informed us that they were desperate men and bushwhackers and that we must hurry out of the country. Fully satisfying himself that the unwelcome visitors were gone, he kindly volunteered his services to pilot us out of immediate danger. Without coat or hat, through the dreary woods of the desolate battle ground, he led the way, the cold wind playing with his long, thin, and almost white hair, making a picture I cannot forget. After walking some distance through this silence and desolation, a point was reached where I remembered to have been once before. He then gave us a parting blessing and slowly turned toward his home, we hurrying on in the direction of Purdy, the home of the noted Colonel Hurst.

A few days more, and our long journey was ended. We at last reached the forks of the road not far from the home of my boy comrade, where I bade him good-by after a weary pilgrimage of more than four hundred miles, much of the way through pathless woods and over rugged mountains, riding one Sunday on a wagon at a dollar a mile. The name of this youthful soldier has gone from my memory. Is he living? Who can tell? Wounded in the army, disabled, and discharged from service, I reached my home, not far from Lexington, Tenn., in February, 1864, the remainder of the trip being made in safety. Home, sweet home! Father, mother, the younger children were there. The wandering boy knows the joy of being once more at home. It was a great surprise to them, for when last heard of I was wounded at Chickamauga. No other tidings reached them until I walked into their presence that dark, snowy evening. That happy meeting can be compared only to the meeting that awaits the faithful in the "home beyond the skies." I had only a few days at home, as my furlough had already expired. Mounted and well clad, I turned my face southward. Forrest had defeated General Smith and driven him back to Memphis. To Lieutenant Day I carried a letter and a pair of socks from his good wife, whom I met on my way South.

The half has not been told of what happened while I was running the gauntlet on that furlough.

BILL ARP's "LETTER TO LINCOLN."—Mr. Lincoln, sir, have you any late news from Harper's Ferry? I heard that Stone W. Jackson kept the parole for a few days and that about fourteen thousand crossed over in twenty-four hours. He is a smart ferryman, sure. Do your folks know how to make it pay? It's a bad crossing, but I suppose it is a heap safer than Ball's Bluff or Shepherdstown.

JACKSON'S WINTER CAMPAIGN IN 1862.

BY P. S. HAGY, ABINGDON, VA.

Thrilling transactions of long ago stand out in memory as a silhouette against the flight of time, and so also the unusual that bring about great suffering and distress to the participants of an event. Doubtless there was no episode during the War between the States that entailed more real acute bodily suffering and discomfort to the troops engaged therein than that of General Jackson's winter campaign in 1862. The result of this campaign and the suffering and fatality following many of the troops by exposure will justify no favorable verdict in its behalf. Neither can it be said that good generalship marked its conception or its execution. Its intent was on a sound basis, if we take no note of the ability of the South to ward off the impending bolts of war in preparation and known to be accumulating at all accessible points to hurl against us at the opening of the season of activity that was so near at hand. With the large number of troops called into service by President Lincoln's proclamation and their almost unlimited resources to draw from, common prudence seemingly ought to have dictated a careful husbanding and careful preparation in every conceivable way to have the troops of the South in as good condition to prove efficient in the defense of their country at the needed hour, rather than to have exposed unseasoned troops to the rigor of a North Virginia midwinter campaign. Its successful execution under the unfavorable influences attending it was a moral impossibility, and the eclat to be hoped for in an expedition of the kind was lost. Let us contemplate what would have happened at Kernstown only a few weeks later if General Jackson had had with him the per cent of troops lost in this winter expedition. This was the opening battle of the season, when and where, with 2,742 infantry, a few cavalry, and two or three batteries of artillery, he had at one time the 11,000 of the enemy defeated; but the grave and the hospital give the answer. This article will deal more in stubborn facts than willful criticism in recording the incidents of this memorable campaign.

The first day of January, 1862, opened as one of the prettiest, warm and balmy, the atmosphere charged with the redolence of yet lingering flowers. The temperature lulled into confidence the unsuspecting soldier, who, when called upon to march, stripped himself of blanket, extra clothing, and, indeed, all extras, and placed them in the baggage wagon, to be retrieved by him at the time of need. On this morning General Jackson mustered the troops he had gathered around Winchester, in Frederick County, Va., his command in all arms numbering close to ten thousand men, and started northwest on the Pewtown Road for some point, his closest friends did not know where. After passing Pewtown he turned his column to the northeast and advanced toward Bath (now Berkeley Springs), in Morgan County. After a march of eighteen or twenty miles the troops went into camp, expecting their baggage wagons to come up. The crowded condition of the road, caused by advancing troops, rendered it impossible for the most of the wagons to pass along in time to find their different commands; therefore a large per cent of the army were destitute of tents, blankets, provisions, and every comfort and necessity the wagons contained; and, to add to their discomfort, the weather had undergone a change, turning cold and threatening rain or snow, making it impossible for the troops to secure comfort except by keeping up fires during the night, a task difficult to do even in a timbered country without axes, while hunger and the lack of natural rest showed the effect it was having upon the temper of the troops. Some few wagons got through early in the morning, relieving some of the commands, but they were exceptions. General Jackson was relentless and ordered the troops forward. While passing along the road, it is said, he came up with the Stonewall Brigade, whose wagons had come up that morning, and the men were cooking their breakfast. He approached General Garnett, who had succeeded him in command of the brigade, and wanted to know the reason of his delay.

"I have halted to let the men cook rations, General," was Garnett's reply. "There is no time for that," replied Jackson briefly. "But it is impossible for the men to march farther without them." "I never found anything impossible with that brigade," answered Jackson in his curtest tone. (J. Esten Cooke, page 90.)

As the day advanced the intensity of the weather became greater. By noon it was raining, and by night it was sleeting and freezing. The command was now approaching Bath, and after the turn of the evening Jackson found his advance guard, a portion of the 48th Virginia under Colonel Campbell, fiercely attacked by a strong body of the enemy posted behind fences and other shelter, from which they poured into the Confederates advancing a fire of considerable volume, but doing little execution. The enemy held their ground until reënforcements were brought up under Colonel Patton, when they fell back on their main body, leaving in the Confederates' hands twenty or more prisoners. This transaction took place a considerable distance in front of Bath and terminated just at dark, when the army went into camp for the second night, the wagons again failing to get to the relief of a large portion of the commands, who were still without food, shelter, or axes, the severity of the weather still increasing.

As night came on it sleeted and froze, so that everything, as well as the ground, was covered with ice the next morning, rendering the condition of many of the troops very distressing. Under this unfavorable condition Jackson's word was, "Press forward!" The army broke camp and started for the town, and on its approach the enemy made a precipitate retreat, running over a body of militia General Jackson had sent around in their rear to intervene between them and the river. Colonel Ashby followed with his cavalry, and the enemy, after removing the impediments in his rear, showed a disposition to dispute the ground before crossing the river, when some cannonading ensued. The enemy retained his position during the day and at night recrossed the Potomac River by wading, the night being severely cold.

The enemy left considerable supplies, which proved quite acceptable to the hungry troops. Among other things which they abandoned in their hurry to get away were a number of fine uniforms, which were appropriated by Confederate officers. Many camp luxuries also fell into the hands of the Confederates and much of the plunder which had been gathered from the citizens of the surrounding country. General Jackson, leaving Bath the morning of the 5th, drew his army up in front of Hancock on the Maryland side, the river between them. The town was occupied at the time by General Lander with a considerable force. General Jackson placed his artillery in position to open on the town, after which he sent forward a flag of truce by General Ashby demanding its surrender. On refusal of the summons Jackson again sent the flag of truce with the statement that he would give them two hours to remove the women and children out of danger, and at the end of that time he would put his artillery in action against the city if not surrendered. Much stir was noticeable in the town. At the expiration of the time limit General Jackson directed his artillery on that part of the town occupied by the enemy. The Federal batteries replying, a brisk cannonade lasted for some time. When it died down for the day, no material damage had been done on either side. The next day the cannonading was resumed, but soon again ceased. This ended the attack on Hancock, but a considerable amount of stores left by the detachment of Federal troops stationed on the south side of the river fell into Confederate hands.

From this point an expedition under Colonel Rust—composed of his regiment, the 3d Arkansas, one other regiment, and a battery—was sent against the Baltimore and Ohio Railroad with instructions to destroy the railroad bridge over Capon River and do as much other damage to the railroad as their means would admit. This service was performed by the destruction of the bridge and the tearing up of much of the road, which proved of great disadvantage for a time to the Federals, it being the main artery of travel westward from Washington City. This service done, the detachment rejoined the main army in front of Hancock. General Jackson remained in front of Hancock until he removed all the captured stores and then turned his course toward Romney, in Hampshire County, where General Kelley was posted with a Federal army estimated at from six to eight thousand men.

By this time General Jackson had divested his mind of the eclat of a surprise, for his movement had become necessarily slow on account of the continued severe weather, and news travels faster than a half frozen army can or will. The country was under a glaze of ice and snow. There had been moderation of the atmosphere enough to dampen the snow, followed by weather below zero, so heavy a crust of ice forming as often to bear up the entire train of army wagons. It was with the greatest uncertainty that the regimental wagons would or could come to us, let the distance be ever so short between camps. It is related that it took from daylight until 3 P.M. for one train of wagons and artillery to pass one hill point.

"The difficulties of the march were fourfold for the trains and artillery. The roads were covered with ice two inches thick and so thoroughly glazed by the sleet that horses and men kept their feet only by the greatest exertion. Men were slipping and their guns going off along the line. Thousands fell flat every day, and both men and animals were often seriously hurt. The knees and muzzles of the horses were terribly injured, and they were seen limping along, crippled and streaming with blood; but still Jackson continued his march. Wagon after wagon slid off the steep and slippery roads and turned bottom upwards despite every attempt made to steady them." (Cooke, page 93.)

General Jackson was everywhere along the line, giving encouragement and often set the example of imparting physical help to a stalled wagon or a disheartened horse. The heartrending scenes that sometimes rose to view and frequently placed before us by the suffering of the people in that part of the country in which these movements took place was feelingly touching. It appeared at times that the Federal soldier esteemed it his duty to kill and destroy and do all damage possible to the weak and defenseless, leaving alone to them their woes as a heritage to linger with them. Nothing was too sacred for them to defile and destroy, and no tender human attachment that bound together family circles was

a safeguard in the hearts of some miserable wretches who were a curse and terror to the inhabitants of this section.

One noted regiment which figured in this part of the country and left a trail of blood and misery the 37th Virginia had the pleasure of meeting at Kernstown, with a stone wall between them, and there and then gave them such a castigation that the 5th Ohio, it was reported, became almost an unorganized force. It was reported that at a large tanyard these marauders shot the man of the house, he falling in his doorway, after which they put the family, consisting of wife and children, out without the privilege of taking anything with them and burned the house over the man. They then killed every domestic thing on the place. This writer counted twenty-two fat hogs that were killed and left in their pen, milch cows, dogs, cats—indeed, there was no domestic thing left alive, the horses and poultry no doubt being appropriated to their use. The tanyard was burned, as well as every outhouse on the premises. At one point on the road for a space of seven miles every house, outhouse, and barn was burned and nothing left to indicate that the country had been inhabited but their ruins.

Having accomplished the feat of clearing Morgan County of the enemy, General Jackson then directed his course toward Romney, in Hampshire County. Falling back to Unger's store, he sent his sick to the hospital at Winchester and then pushed forward by way of Slane's Crossroads, crossing Great Capon River, and finally arrived at Romney with a much-exhausted army. The enemy, under General Kelley, first determined to hold and defend the town, but finally withdrew in a panic and fled across the Potomac River, leaving in the Confederate hands a considerable amount of stores.

As to the composition of the troops led by Jackson in this expedition, a little light thrown thereon will elucidate and explain the feeling that existed between him and Gen. W. W. Loring and also entertained by the different portions of the army originally commanded by each in their separate spheres. Like all unnecessaries, it proved an evil to the service. It was understood that the two generals had equal authority in the management of the expedition, and this proved an evil, for Jackson ignored it, and a feeling of estrangement arose between the two generals that was participated in by the subaltern officers and the privates. J. Esten Cook says: "Jackson was regarded as a man of weak judgment and deficient intellect, who accidentally attained his position, and the report was industriously circulated that he cared nothing for the men of Loring's command. With this the camp had buzzed at Winchester, and the hardships of the winter expedition had added virulence to the sentiment."

General Loring was a West Point graduate and had attained a favorable reputation for military skill in the war with Mexico. After General Garnett was killed on the Laurel Hill retreat, he was sent up to take command of the Confederate troops in that mountainous region. He stood in high favor with the troops, and in a short time they began to idolize him. When in December, 1861, he was ordered with a large portion of his force to Winchester, in the Valley of Virginia, the two favorite generals were brought together, the Loring forces outnumbering those General Jackson already had at that point. Friction between the two forces soon began to crop out, as well as between the two commanders, and this spirit between them lasted until the activities of the spring campaigns began and Jackson proved his great ability as a military leader. Romney was in Confederate hands, but the Federals yet had control of a part of

Hampshire County. Some skirmishing between detachments of the opposing forces took place, but no action of magnitude occurred. The 37th Virginia, with the 3d Arkansas Regiment, all under Colonel Rust, was reconnoitering toward Little Capon Bridge when it fell into ambuscade by the enemy at night posted across and along the railroad. A sharp skirmish ensued, the enemy soon yielding in retreat, after some casualties, to the Confederates. In John O. Casler's "Four Years in the Stonewall Brigade," page 64, is given a good summing up of the results of the campaign: "We were out nearly one month and had miserable weather all the time and did no fighting except some little skirmishing, but we lost more men from sickness than if we had been engaged in a big battle. We accomplished nothing, for the enemy retreated across the Potomac, only to come back again as soon as we left. Winchester was full of soldiers sick with pneumonia, and they died by the hundreds."

The results of the campaign were such as could be accomplished. General Jackson could only hope that the ground he had retrieved from the enemy would remain so. In this he was doomed to disappointment, for this very section of country proved to be a ground of contention until the Confederates were forced from the country. To appearances all had been done that had been planned for at the beginning, and it had come to the time to arrange the results gained. To do this the Stonewall Brigade was ordered to return to their winter quarters at Winchester and the Loring Division ordered to remain at Romney and police that and the surrounding country. This arrangement seemed to suit General Jackson and the Stonewall Brigade all right; but it must be remembered that where there are two parties it takes the two to make a contract. It was claimed to be wholly one-sided by the Loring view, and they alleged that General Jackson was "taking care of his pets"; so steps were at once taken to enter their complaint and lay the matter before the authorities at Richmond. The result was that only a few days elapsed before orders came to General Loring from the Richmond authorities to fall back with his command on Winchester, which place they reached on the 7th of February. Much adverse feeling was engendered on both sides, and the action of the Richmond authorities caused General Jackson to resign his position in the army; and it was only by much persuading that the country did not lose his valuable services afterwards.

What a perfect mirror time is, and how clearly is shown the duty of men in after years, when it is too late!

THE REAL NATION.

There was a time when nations came to be
Because they were locked in from sea to sea,
Because they lay between great mountain ranges high,
Because a people spoke one language commonly,
Because they claimed one common worship-creed,
Because they were of but one race, one breed,
Because some institution held them true—
The Church, the army, or the union—through
Peculiar mode of living, government. But none
Of these things count, when all is said and done,
For perpetuity in any nation's life; there needs must be
A greater element, a purpose grounded in real unity;
There must be underneath and over all that strong,
True, vital principle, unselfishness, which lives
For service to the race, which grows because it gives.
    —D. G. Bickers, in Macon Telegraph.

A GEORGIA COMMAND IN ACTIVE SERVICE.

BY JOHN W. HIGGINS, GRAPEVINE, TEX.

On April 20, 1861, I enlisted from Dade County, Ga., in Company B, known as the "Lookout Infantry," which became a part of the 6th Georgia Regiment of Infantry, A. H. Colquitt being our first colonel. We reached Richmond, Va., on the 31st of May. From there we were ordered to Yorktown and got there on the 3d of June, 1861, remaining there under drill until April, 1862.

When McClellan's army laid siege to Yorktown on the 4th or 5th of May, Gen. Joseph E. Johnston being in command, we evacuated the place and fell back up the Peninsula westward toward Richmond. McClellan's army overtaking our rear guard forced us to stand and give battle at Williamsburg, the old colonial capital of Virginia.

Johnston's attack on the west wing of the Federal army on May 31, 1862, resulted in the battle of Seven Pines, in which battle our company had a total of fifty-five men, nine of whom were killed on the field and nineteen were wounded, of whom a number died later. All of these casualties of Company B took place in about seven minutes.

General Johnston having been wounded on the 31st, Gen. Robert E. Lee was assigned to the command of this army on the 2d of June, 1862. On the 26th of June he attacked the right wing of the Federal army. The fighting continued for seven days, my company participating in four of the seven battles: Mechanicsville, Cold Harbor, White Oak Swamp, and Malvern Hill. In the battle of Cold Harbor my company lost six killed and sixteen wounded, and a few were wounded in the other three battles, but none were killed. At Malvern Hill my regiment was under Stonewall Jackson and fought on the left center of Jackson's Corps. My regiment reached the top of the hill three times, but in each instance we were repulsed and driven back. Very soon after the battle the Confederate army began to move north to meet the Federal army under Pope, and on August 9 a considerable battle ensued, in which Jackson defeated Pope. The two armies maneuvered for several days, Jackson finally moving around the west wing of Pope's army, taking position between this west wing and Washington City at Manassas; and there on the 28th, 29th, and 30th of August he fought the second battle of Manassas and expelled the Federal army from the field, it retreating into Washington.

In the meantime the Confederate army marched into Maryland by the fords of the Potomac River and took possession of Frederick. From this point General Jackson was detached from this army to capture, if possible, Harper's Ferry, D. H. Hill and other commands engaging McLoud's army at South Mountain to keep McClellan from approaching Jackson's rear, all of which resulted in the fall of Harper's Ferry on the 15th of September, 1862. After this General Lee concentrated his army at or near Sharpsburg, and in the battle of Sharpsburg, on September 17, 1862, my regiment lost six officers in command, all being killed. The seventh commander of this regiment was wounded and taken prisoner on the field. My company's loss in this battle was six killed and about eighteen or nineteen wounded. I and two others were the only surviving members present and able for service when the battle closed. Lee's army remained on the field confronting the enemy until the early night of September 18, when we began to fall back and recrossed the Potomac into Virginia.

At this stage of the war General Burnside superseded McClellan as commander of the Army of the Potomac and at once began his move on to Richmond via Fredericksburg; but Lee concentrated his army in front of Burnside and defeated him on the 13th of December, 1862, at Fredericksburg, forcing the Federals to recross the Rappahannock River. After this Burnside was superseded by General Hooker, who recrossed the Rappahannock in the last days of April and early in May and was attacked and defeated by General Lee with only about two-thirds of his army, three divisions of Longstreet's Corps being absent in Southeast Virginia. This was the battle of Chancellorsville, where the great Jackson was wounded.

After this battle Colquitt's Brigade, of which the 6th Georgia was a part, was detached from the Army of Northern Virginia and sent South to Kinston, N. C., from which point we were transferred to Charleston, S. C., and fought the enemy on James Island on the 16th of July, 1863, forcing them back under cover of their gunboats. We then garrisoned James Island and Battery Wagner on Morris Island and Fort Sumter until the 9th of February, 1864, at which time we were put aboard cars and sent to Savannah and from there on to Florida, meeting Seymour's army on the 20th of that month in the battle of Olustee, or Ocean Pond, driving him back to Jacksonville. The casualties of my company in this short but hotly contested battle were eight killed, only a few being wounded. Soon after this battle we marched north through the Ocanoca Swamps, striking the Gulf and Savannah Railroad, over which we were again transferred to Virginia, getting to Drewry's Bluff in time to participate in that battle on the 16th of May, 1864.' Three regiments of Colquitt's Division, my regiment being one of them, were held in reserve in the beginning of the fight, finally being sent to the extreme left to assist Gracie's Brigade; and we turned the enemy's right from the James River, doubling it back and driving it to the westward on or toward their center. During this fighting through the woods a six- or eight-pound shell burst over us, wounding sixteen men. I was among the number; but, finding my wounds not serious, I continued on with my company throughout the entire engagement. In this fight our ammunition became exhausted, and we were ordered to lie down and seek such shelter as the surroundings afforded. Four of us took shelter behind one small tree, and my three comrades were wounded, while I escaped unscathed. After this battle Butler retreated, under the protection of his gunboats, to Bermuda Hundred, where we besieged him for about two weeks, when he withdrew from his position across the James and joined Meade's army on the left.

Very soon after this we crossed the James River on pontoon bridges and joined Lee's right on the old battle field of Cold Harbor on June 1, and there on the 3d of June we fought the second battle of Cold Harbor, in which the lines of battle were some eighteen or nineteen miles long. The enemy rushed our position early in the morning and succeeded in breaking our line in two places. We regained the lost ground at one point early in the fight, but failed to entirely regain the other point. This battle, to my mind, was the bloodiest of the entire war, the dead lying in heaps in front of our position. I might except the fight at Spottsylvania C. H. on the 12th of May, 1864, when Grant asked permission three different times to bury his dead, which was granted; and yet quite a number of the boys in blue were left to be buried by us.

About the 11th or 12th of June Grant withdrew from our front, crossed the James River, and attacked Petersburg. Colquitt's Brigade was ordered to Petersburg, arriving there on the night of June 16, when the siege of Petersburg properly began; and our brigade was on the firing line at various points almost daily until the 28th of September, 1864. On the 19th of August we were in the battle on the Weldon Railroad and then back to the ditches again until September 28, when Colquitt was ordered across the James to take back Fort Harrison. On the 30th of September the following brigade commanders were ordered to do this work by a concerted attack: Colquitt and Clingman in center, Denning and Anderson on left, and Martin and Haygood on right. But by some miscarriage or misconception of the plans the effort to retake this fort failed, resulting in a number of our men being taken prisoners, the writer among the number. I was carried to Point Lookout and held until June 27, 1865, when I was paroled and furnished free transportation to Chattanooga, Tenn. I am now seventy-five years old and still think I fought in a just cause.

STEELE'S ESCAPE AT JENKINS'S FERRY.

BY C. J. HANKS, GERMANTOWN, TENN.

In his article in the VETERAN of December, page 545, P. S. Hagy is badly off in regard to General Steele. No doubt it was the intention of Steele and Banks to unite at Shreveport; but after leaving Little Rock General Steele had reached Camden, Ark., on his march to meet Banks when he learned that the latter had been beaten by General Taylor. Steele started back to Little Rock by way of Pine Bluff. Comrade Hagy says Steele was met at Jenkins Ferry, on Sabine River. He was not met at Jenkins Ferry, but was overtaken there by General Price. (Jenkins Ferry is on the Saline River; there is no Sabine River in Arkansas.) The Saline River is a small stream, probably fifty yards wide, between the Arkansas and Ouachita Rivers. I was on General Churchill's staff at the time and was in the battle with him. I belonged on Gen. Dandridge McRae's staff, but had gone South with him from Jackson, Woodruff County, where we had been recruiting. Having no command of his own, he volunteered on General Price's staff and I on General Churchill's.

It had been raining for a day or two, and the roads were in a terrible condition. The battle took place in the Saline River bottom, which was so boggy that neither side could use artillery; so it was purely a small arms fight. The Confederates ran one battery on the field, but it was practically useless on account of the soft ground of the river bottom.

It seemed that the fortune of war favored Steele at this time. Had we been able to come up with him a few hours earlier, we could probably have captured his army, as we could also have crossed the river; or if he had been a few hours later the river would have been out of its banks, and he could not have crossed. As it was, the river was just bank full, and he had just time to cross on a pontoon, which he destroyed as soon as he was over; and as we had no pontoon, he made his escape. He was encumbered by a great many negroes with every kind of vehicle and all kinds of plunder taken by them. The last of Steele's troops to cross the river were negroes, and this was the first time I had met any negro troops. I think Steele's idea was to sacrifice his negroes if necessary to save his white troops. It was a very severe fight and cost us some fine officers and a good many men. The fight lasted for some three or four hours or more. We had with us the cavalry of Generals Fagan and Marmaduke.

IN THE YEAR 1861.

COMPILED BY JOHN C. STILES, BRUNSWICK, GA.

VOLUME I., "OFFICIAL RECORDS."

Maj. Robert Anderson, of Sumter Fame.—A Southern writer said that as Major Anderson was born in the noble old "dark and bloody ground" of Kentucky he would be found on the side of the South when the Union was dismembered. But he stayed with the Union and made about as large a commotion in the rest of the war as a ripple caused by a stone thrown into the Atlantic.

Americans as Fighters.—General Beauregard said that two thousand Americans ought to beat twice that number of any troops trying to land in Charleston Harbor. He evidently did not class the Yankees as Americans.

Floating Battery Constructed by Confederates.—The floating battery intended to breach the walls of Sumter went ashore and is now a fixed fortification. This was, I think, the first effort in history of such a weapon.

A Rash Boast.—Governor Moore, of Louisiana, said: "The people of Louisiana are one and cannot be subdued." He changed his mind later, however.

C. S. A. Bounty First on Record.—A bounty of $30 was *promised* all men who enlisted in the regular army of the Confederacy. Note that "promised" is in italics.

Extraordinary Cannon.—Governor Pickens, of South Carolina, tells of the arrival of a fine gun that threw a shell with the accuracy of a dueling pistol on a charge of only one and one-half pounds of powder. Evidently powder had more force in those days than at the present.

Cartridge Bags.—General Whiting reports from Wilmington: "I have started the ladies making cartridge bags, and that keeps their little hearts quiet." And that was going some.

Confederacy Recognized by the United States.—General Bragg said that the blockade of Pensacola was an acknowledgment of the national existence and independence of the Confederacy. Whether they did recognize our independence, I am not sure, but before they tackled us many times I am certainly sure they at least recognized that we were some belligerents.

Cotton as Breastworks.—General Ripley states that one shot from the enemy entered an embrasure, but that no damage was done, as it was stopped by a bale of cotton. This idea was probably taken from Old Hickory's defense of New Orleans, where, it is said, he had cotton bales and molasses puncheons to slow the Britishers up. I would judge that a molasses cask hit by a cannon ball would make a hideous mess.

First Death Consequent of the War.—On January 26 Thaddeus S. Strawinski, aged eighteen years, private in the Columbia Artillery, South Carolina Troops, was accidently killed by a shot from a revolver. So a ball was started with the youth of the South.

Spoiling for a Fight.—A gentleman in Pensacola wails that the troops are dispirited by inaction, despondent at the thought of never having a fight; only in for twelve months, but want a place for the war. And they got it both ways from the middle.

C. S. A. Flag First Under Fire.—General Beauregard sent the flag that waved over Moultrie to the War Department, saying that as it was the first Confederate flag ever under fire he thought it worthy preserving. That flag had three shots through it.

South Carolina Flags.—Morris Island batteries floated a red flag with a white palmetto and Fort Moultrie a white one with a green palmetto. South Carolinians will have to say which was the official color.

Florida Looking Out for Herself.—Governor Perry tells the War Department that two thousand men are needed for the defense of the State, and if "We are to take care of ourselves say so." And they came mighty near having to do it too.

C. S. A. Fuses.—General Beauregard writes from Charleston that the shells sent cannot be used, as there were no fuses with them. Same old story happened all through the war.

Frightful Hardships.—A Confederate officer during the siege of Fort Sumter reported: "In the midst of the greatest exposure to the most inclement weather (in the month of April) many were bivouacking in the open air without any covering; many more sheltered by wide burrows in the sand hills; not a murmur of complaint was made." Wasn't it awful as compared to Petersburg and other salubrious places later in the war?

Fall of New Orleans Foretold.—General Beauregard predicted that one steamer with two or three big guns could go up to New Orleans and in a few hours lay the city under a forced contribution of millions of dollars. Which was done in a way.

Ranges of Firing at Fort Sumter.—Fort Moultrie to Sumter, 1,900 yards; Fort Johnson, to Sumter, 2,450 yards; Morris Island to Sumter, 2,400 yards. With the guns of to-day at these ranges it would be like shooting birds on the ground.

Search Lights.—General Beauregard reports that the Drummond lights had arrived, but no operator with them. To the Confederacy, I think, belongs the honor of the first use of these powerful aids to warfare.

The First Shot of the War.—The first shot of the war was fired on January 9 by South Carolina troops against the steamer Star of the West, and, as Captain Foster, U. S. A., puts it, "Thus the war was started." Whoever pulled the lanyard certainly had the satisfaction of realizing that he had started something.

The First Shot Fired at Fort Sumter.—The first shot fired at Fort Sumter was fired by the venerable Edward Ruffin, who begged that honor. He evidently was a bloody-minded "venerable."

Shot Penetration.—Major Anderson reported that the greatest penetration made in the walls of Sumter by any one shot was twenty-two inches. Comparisons of this and the penetration of the European "Jack Johnsons" of to-day are odious.

Red-Hot Shot.—Major Anderson says: "As soon as the flames burst from the fort the enemy's batteries redoubled their fire with red-hot shot from most of their guns." We got the start on them with burning, but the man who made war what he is supposed to have called it made our efforts appear puerile in that line.

VOLUME II., "OFFICIAL RECORDS."

Waste of Ammunition.—General Lee issued a circular to the effect that one man had been killed and several wounded by the reckless waste of ammunition around the camps and *hoped* that the troops would pay regard to the importance of economizing their supply, so vital at all times. That was General Lee's fault; he invariably hoped, wished, or trusted instead of demanding.

Confederate Veteran.

81

Well Armed.—A Virginia gentleman wrote President Davis that, although he already had three sons in the army, he himself would personally take the field armed with rifle, shotgun, pistol, and cutlass and relying upon the God of battles, go to meet the enemy. That gentleman was almost equal to a brigade later in the war.

Failure of Confederates to Advance After Bull Run.—General Beauregard said: "An army which had fought as ours did that day against uncommon odds, under a July sun, most of the time without water, and without food except a hastily snatched meal at dawn, was not in condition for the toil of an eager and effective pursuit of an enemy immediately after the battle. On the following day a heavy rain intervened to obstruct our advance with reasonable prospects of success and, added to this the want of cavalry force of sufficient numbers, made an efficient pursuit a military impossibility." That settles the question. He was there and also certainly a military man of great ability.

Any Cause if Sustained Is Just.—General Patterson, U. S. A., tells Colonel Townsend: "The moral force of a just cause, sustained by a strong and equable government, will conquer." He was right. If the government is strong enough, any cause, whether just or unjust, will conquer.

Chaplain Wanted.—A Virginia colonel of cavalry reported to the War Department that of sabers his command had few and wanted no more, as he much preferred hatchets as a cavalry weapon. He also asked for a chaplain, saying that having a fully commissioned and authenticated man of God attached to his command, aside from the positive good done, would tend to dispel some of the unenviable soubriquets preferred against his regiment. He needed a man of God to offset those scalping hatchets.

Militant Clergyman.—A South Carolina colonel, in his report of the battle of Bull Run, mentions particularly the gallant conduct of a clergyman, whose rifle did good service. This goes to show that "a man's a man for a' that" and reminds us of the stuttering parson captain of a battery, who, unable to say fire, told the gunner to "shoot the damn thing."

Southern Copperheads.—Gen. Henry A. Wise, of Virginia, told General Cooper: "We are treading on snakes while aiming at the enemy. The grass of the soil we are defending is full of copperhead traitors." I had thought that this reptile was confined to the North, but this proves that some of them had slipped over the border.

Jefferson Davis Compared to an Army.—General Scott, U. S. A., told General McDowell that "Mr. Jefferson Davis, or the enemy, is advancing against you. Rally and compact your troops to meet any emergency." General Scott surely had a wholesome respect for our President, even if he did call him "Mister," and at that he did more than General Beauregard, who called President Lincoln "Abraham."

Freezing for a Fight.—A spy told General McDowell a few days before the Bull Run fight that, of the Southern army, the South Carolinians were better armed and equipped and "freezing for a fight." They got what they wanted, and if anybody fought better than they did it is not on record.

Only One Confederate Flag Captured in Bull Run Campaign.—Colonel Heintzelman, U. S. A., reported that his command picked up a secession flag at Fairfax Station and adds that it was the only one captured in the campaign. If the list of "medals-of-honor" holders, U. S. A., is consulted, it will be seen that this is also the only Confederate flag captured that a medal was not issued for.

Hurrah for Georgia!—President Davis tells Gen. Joseph E. Johnston that "Georgia tenders men for any length of service and to go anywhere." And it did the same thing all through the war.

Grapevine News.—A deserter tells General Davis, U. S. A., that Gen. R. E. Lee is opposing him at Blackburn's Ford. General Patterson is told that Ben McCulloch, with a brigade of Texas sharpshooters, is approaching Harper's Ferry. General McClellan is informed that Albert S. Johnston is marching into West Virginia with a large force. Which goes to show that "all's fair in love and war."

A Hell Snorter.—A captain of Virginia cavalry reports that when he came in sight of the enemy: "I walked my horse out into the clearing in plain view and when not more than twenty paces from them picked out the commanding officer and shot him dead in his tracks. The whole party then yelled, 'Look out for the d— Virginia horsemen,' and at once fled. I rode into them at full speed, giving at the same time a loud 'Walla-Walla' war whoop, and then delivered my second shot, which brought another man to the ground dead. I shot the first through the heart and the other under the right shoulder blade. My third shot missed a man, but killed a sorrel mule. I fired only three times." From the above we deduce: First, that the captain was one of the army corps of descendants of Pocahontas on account of his war cry; secondly, that, although his third shot missed a man, he got considerable of that delicacy that was later in the war worth its weight in gold in Vicksburg; and, thirdly, that he was running a close second to the hero of San Juan Hill during the "Yanko-Spanko" War in 1898.

Modesty.—Another captain of Virginia cavalry, in his report of the Bull Run affair, says: "As to the number killed by my command, I decline speaking, but I know it was very considerable." He doesn't remind us of the man that killed the mule.

Proclamations.—It is said that the art of oratory died in the sixties, and I must confess that the following extracts from proclamations of Southern leaders are a cut above anything that I have ever heard: "Men of Virginia! Men of Kanawha! To arms! The enemy has invaded your soil. Rise and strike for your firesides and altars. Repel the aggressors and preserve your honor and your rights. Come to the aid of your fathers, brothers, and comrades for the protection of your mothers, wives, and sisters." Good! "A reckless and unprincipled tyrant has invaded your soil. Abraham Lincoln has thrown his abolition hosts among you. Their war cry is 'Beauty and booty.' Your honor and that of your wives and daughters, your fortunes and your lives are involved in this momentous conflict." Better! "The North has not openly and according to the usage of civilized nations declared war on us. We make no war on them; but should Virginia soil be polluted by the tread of a single man in arms from north of the Potomac, it will cause open war. Men of the Potomac border, to arms! Your country calls you to her defense. Already you have in spirit responded. You await but the order to march, to rendezvous, to defend your State, your liberty, and your homes. Women of Virginia, cast from your arms all cowards and breathe the pure and holy, the high and glowing inspiration of your nature into the hearts and souls of lover, husband, brother, father, and friend. Almighty God, Author and Governor of the world, thou Source of all life, truth, justice and power, be thou our God, be thou with us, then shall we fear not a world against us." Best!

Didn't Appreciate Being Shot At.—A captain of Virginia troops in Alexandria reported that his videttes were fired upon and forced to seek shelter, as the balls struck trees close to their post, and he further says that he demanded an explanation from the corporal of the United States forces opposite to them. These men never did get over not liking to be shot at, but they at least afterwards never asked for an apology.

VOLUME III., "OFFICIAL RECORDS."

Breastworks of Hemp.—Gen. Sterling Price, commonly known as "Old Pap," reported that in the battle of Lexington, Mo., bales of hemp were successfully used as movable breastworks. Later in the war the owners of this commodity asked to be paid for same, but history fails to show with what success.

Irish Flag Captured at Belmont from the Confederates.—A Union colonel reported that his regiment captured a fine large flag, decorated with the "Harp of Erin" on a green silk ground. Which goes to show that, as usual in most wars, Pat fought cheerfully on both sides of the question.

Grapevine News.—Gen. Leonidas Polk writes: "We have heard from Virginia that Lee has met and defeated Rosecrans and taken almost the whole of his command prisoners." But the shoe was on the other foot.

Proclamation.—The following order issued by General Polk after the battle of Belmont shows that the Bishop was some talker as well as fighter: "The major general commanding, with profound acknowledgment of the overruling providence of Almighty God, congratulates the army under his command on the glorious victory achieved on the 7th of November. The battle began under disadvantages which would have discouraged veteran troops, yet the obstinate resistance offered by a handful of men to an overwhelming force must long be a lesson to them, and the closing scenes of the day, in which a routed enemy was vigorously pursued, will ever be remembered in connection with that spirit of our people which has proclaimed in triumphant tones upon every battle field: 'We can and will be free.'" But Providence willed it otherwise.

Didn't Like Their Rations.—Some Arkansas troops were complaining of the rations, or rather lack of them, which brought forth the following salty remarks from the issuing officer: "You Arkansas men can live on beef alone and then live better than you ever lived at home. You can do the same as Missourians; and in a war of liberty coffee, sugar, and rice are not indispensable." They fought later and mighty well at that on heap worse than beef.

Flowery Report.—A Missouri general, in his report of the Lexington fight, said: "All the men under my command acted with a patience, courage, and endurance worthy only of the cause engaged in. For more than fifty hours they lay there panting like hounds in summer when they scent the stately deer; eager not for revenge, but to teach again the minions of the tyrant that Missouri shall be free." But—.

Retaliation.—A Missouri general issued the following manifesto which was brought forth by an order issued by the Union general, Fremont, sometimes called the "Path Finder," which name was very appropriate when Stonewall Jackson got in behind him in the Valley of Virginia later in the war: "Whereas General Fremont, commanding the minions of Abraham Lincoln in the State of Missouri, has threatened to shoot any citizen-soldier found in arms within certain limits; therefore know ye that I, ———, brigadier general of Mis-souri troops, do most solemnly promise that for every member of the Missouri State Guard who shall be put to death in pursuance of this said order of General Fremont I will hang, draw, and quarter a minion of said Abraham Lincoln." The brigadier would have done it too.

Both Sides Running.—A general of Missouri State troops reported that his cavalry exchanged shots with the enemy, and both sides turned tail and headed for home; and he added that he intended giving his men a good lecture. And I have no doubt that he did.

Sigel's Flying Dutchmen.—General Steele, U. S. A., reported that, in regard to what had been called Sigel's masterly retreat from Springfield, it more resembled a crowd of refugees than an army of organized troops. He put his brigade in the advance, and his rear was brought up by the regulars, and this was the only evidence of skill manifested by him during his memorable retreat. General Halleck said of Sigel that he always had and always would run.

State Troops.—A Missourian wrote the Secretary of War of the Confederate States: "The State troops were all willing to be transferred to the Confederate service, and not a dissent would have been made if the transfer had been made by order without referring to the men. They had been in the army for five months and had never received any pay or clothing; and when it was left to their individual choice, being naked and barefooted, the natural impulse to each individual was, 'I must go home.'" And they went. Ben McCulloch said: "I have made myself very unpopular by speaking to them frequently about the necessity of order and discipline in their organization. A thousand of them were put to flight by a single cannon shot and ran in the greatest confusion without the loss of a single man except one, who died of overheat or sunstroke." I will not mention the State these people came from, but history tells us that some of this class from my State "also ran."

M. Jeff Thompson.—One of the unique figures of the war was Brig. Gen. M. Jeff Thompson, who wrote to General Pillow (by the way, the latter general was also in this class) as follows: "I am working for the cause and am willing to work in any kind of harness and any part of the team, so you do not tie me behind the wagon. You ask me to let you know our condition and wants. The fact is that although my men are in fine spirits, yet we want everything to make them efficient, shoes especially, tin cups, canteens, and several hundred guns. I herewith send you a requisition for a tent for my own use. I have been sleeping about more like a stray dog than a general, and the State of Missouri has not a yard of material suitable for tents or money to buy it with. If you wish a legal excuse to advance, withdraw your control over me for a few hours and then come to my rescue." Both of these generals were unique, but they proved by their acts that the Confederacy had no braver or more patriotic soldiers than they.

Rebel Yell.—General McCulloch, in his report of the battle of Springfield, Mo., says: "Missourians, Arkansans, Louisianians, and Texans pushed forward. The incessant roll of musketry was deafening, and the balls fell thick as hail stones; but still our gallant Southerners pushed onward and, with one wild yell, broke upon the enemy, pushing them back and strewing the ground with their dead." The famous Rebel yell had possibly been heard before, but this is the first instance of its appearance in history

SUFFERING ON THE SOUTHWEST BORDER.

BY MRS. FLORA E. STEVENS, KANSAS CITY, MO.

An article in the January VETERAN on "The South's Suffering" dwells upon the devastation inflicted by Sherman and Sheridan as the greatest endured by the South during the war; but these troops were chivalrous, high-principled men in comparison with the Kansas soldiers and the members of the 2d Colorado in their treatment of the unfortunate dwellers of Missouri on the Kansas border. The Kansas troops, especially the 5th, 6th, and 7th Volunteer Cavalry, came into Missouri solely to murder—i. e., hang and shoot—and to plunder. Trains of wagons filled with household goods, supplies, grain, etc., rolled over the border and thousands of sheep, cattle, and fine horses till the border of Missouri was simply "cleaned out" of everything worth carrying away. They began even before Missouri seceded and made no distinction between Union and Confederate. In the negro cabins at Lawrence, Kans., were many thousand-dollar pianos. Mr. E. Stine, a well-known citizen of Kansas City and a Union man, told me that on one single trip Jennison, the gambler-colonel of the 7th Kansas, crossed into Kansas with a hundred freight wagons loaded with stolen plunder, followed by all kinds of stock and a thousand negroes on foot, whom Jennison was taking into Kansas to form into regiments and send back into Missouri to steal and destroy.

The border was not in favor of secession for itself, for, though Southern and slave-holding and sympathizing with the other States, it feared secession would leave it unprotected, open to the assaults of the entire Northwest. Senator Vest stated that "but one-fifth of the votes cast in 1860 were for the secession candidates." Not a single Kansas soldier had a right to enter Missouri, yet this district bore the most enormous suffering of the entire country in proportion to its extent.

Where else in the South did a United States Senator head a regiment and fall suddenly upon a peaceful hamlet, slay a score of defenseless citizens, and then return with great loads of plunder and stock, boasting that they came but for loot, as did Jim Lane in 1861 in attacking Osceola, Mo.? while even the Western Journal of Commerce, of Kansas City, a black Republican paper, openly accused them of selling blooded horses, stolen from Missouri, on the streets of Leavenworth at twenty-five dollars a head (worth five hundred), adding that "General Lane's own share of the spoil was a fine carriage."

Where else do you find a regiment crossing the State line in covered wagons, as did John T. Burris, of Olathe, Kans., and the 6th Kansas Volunteers, going to Independence, Mo., and back to their homes, every man riding a horse taken from the defenseless Missourians—nine-tenths of them Union—and the wagons, called "Burris's gunboats," loaded with costly spoil? And these raids were repeated again and again upon an unprotected people. After the war Lane committed suicide through remorse for his blood-stained career.

Where else do you find old men and mere boys hanged by the hundreds simply because they or their fathers had come from some seceded State years before?

Where else do you find a general who would pick for his staff such a set of cutthroats that their very name has become a byword, as did Blunt, of the notorious "Red Legs"?

Where else do you find an officer issue an edict that every boy of nineteen years or over who did not join the Union army should be shot, as did at Independence, Mo., William Homer Pennock, of St. Joseph? Where else that old ladies,

feeble, refined, were ordered out into the Red Leg camps to cook for these villains.

In what other State was a woman put in jail for giving a loaf of bread to her own son, a Confederate soldier, as was Mrs. Tarleton, of Jefferson City, mother of Mrs. Phil Chappell, wife of a State Treasurer of Missouri?

In what other State were young girls put in prison or banished from the State by the hundreds for the sole offense of conveying food to their brothers and relatives hiding in the timber to protect them from the negroes?

In what other part of the country were delicate young women sentenced to the penitentiary for humanely aiding Confederates?

In what other part were men hanged for selling corn to Confederates?

Where were Confederates denied burial and their bodies ordered left exposed to be devoured by wolves and vultures, while any who dared bury them were themselves shot?

Where were men killed for feeding Confederates? Where were prisoners shot by the scores?

Where else did men chain ten-year-old girls on the upper floor of a brick building and Union soldiers dig out the foundation beneath till the building fell and killed these girls with infinite torture, as "Bill" Anderson's young sisters were treated by the soldiers in Kansas City in August, 1863?

Where else did a general issue a decree depopulating three counties—Jackson, Clay, and Bates—as did Tom Ewing in August, 1863? And his superior commander, Schofield, said that he "regretted the edict (order No. 11) had not been extended to a fourth county, Lafayette."

In what other State did the legislature forbid men to preach the gospel unless they took oath that they had shown no act of mercy to a Confederate or his family as did the radicals of Missouri in 1864, pass the hideous "ironclad," or "test," oath under which for years honest, kind-hearted ministers were put in jail, fined, and a dozen or more killed, even Union men, because they set God and their conscience above venal lawmakers?

No, people of the South, of the country, for sheer open, gloating, undisguised atrocity toward the helpless give the black honors (?) to the Kansas troops, the "Dutch," part of the Union Missouri militia, a detachment of the 2d Colorado while in the border district of Missouri.

For unexampled suffering, for the highest rank of victims give the supreme place in history and your love and memory to the Southerners of this despoiled country, the northwest outpost of the Confederacy.

THE AVATAR OF HELL.

Six thousand years of commune, God with man,
Two thousand years of Christ; yet from such roots,
Immortal, earth reaps only bitterest fruits.
The fiends rage now as when they first began;
Hate, Lust, Greed, Vanity, triumphant still,
Yell, shout, exult, and lord o'er human will.
The sun moves back. The fond convictions felt
That in the progress of the race we stood,
Two thousand years of height above the flood,
Before the day's experience sink and melt
As frost beneath the fire! And what remains
Of all our grand ideals and great gains,
With Goth, Hun, Vandal warring in their pride,
While the meek Christ is hourly crucified?

—Selected.

THE LAST ROLL

FROM "MEMORIAL ODE."

We read a lesson in God's open Book—
All the fair page with one great text is rife;
And though we run, we yet read in one look
   That death but leads to life.

Thus thinking o'er life's promise-breaking dreams,
Its lights and shadows made of hopes and fears,
I say that death is kinder than he seems
   And not the king of tears.

Why shrink, then, from the tender grave aghast?
Why shed hot tears above its friendly sod?
For is it not in sooth, O friends, the last
   Great charity from God?

Let perfect faith bind up each bleeding heart,
Smile through your tears upon its grassy slope.
Since Christ hath slumbered, may we not depart
   Sustained by Christian hope?
         —*James Barron Hope.*

JAMES A. FISHER.

James Alexander Fisher was a gallant Confederate soldier. He enlisted in Company G, 17th Virginia Regiment of Volunteers, Corse's Brigade, Pickett's Division, Longstreet's Corps, in April, 1861, and served faithfully throughout the war in Virginia, North Carolina, and Pennsylvania. A part of the time he was with Company K. He was wounded on May 16, 1864, in the battle of Drewry's Bluff and sent to Howard Grove Hospital. Six months later he returned to his command and served continuously from that time until discharged at Appomattox in April, 1865.

Comrade Fisher died at Marshall, Mo., on November 17, 1916, and was buried in Ridge Park Cemetery by his comrades of the John S. Marmaduke Camp, No. 554, U. C. V., of which he had long been a member. Fitting resolutions were passed by the Camp in honor of this faithful comrade, of whom it was said that "he was a friend to all, in hearty sympathy with every good and honest effort, and loyal and true to his cause. A Virginian by birth, he was a worthy son of his native and honored State. For forty years he had been a part of the life of his community, where his faithful, unselfish, and sacrificing service as a public official had been above criticism. No appeal was ever made to him in behalf of a worthy cause that did not have his hearty support. Devoted to his family and home, his was an ideal life. His loyalty to the cause of the Confederacy could never be shaken, and no greater pleasure ever came to him than to review the trying experiences of the war. His last days were spent in pleasant reminiscences of the past. * * * Our Camp has lost a faithful member and our community a citizen whose memory will ever be cherished with honor."

DANIEL MURRAY LEE.

Died on his farm, in Stafford County, Va., two miles from Fredericksburg, Va., on December 17, 1916, Daniel Murray Lee, son of Capt. Sidney Smith Lee, of the Confederate States navy, brother of Gen. Fitzhugh Lee, and a nephew of Gen. Robert E. Lee. His mother was the sister of James M. Mason, United States Senator from Virginia and Embassador to England from the Confederate States, who, with Slidell, was captured on the English steamer Trent by United States authorities, who were compelled by the English government to surrender him back to England.

Daniel Lee was a past midshipman in the Confederate States navy and upheld the records of his ancestry. He was at Hampton Roads on the steamer Johnstown March 8 and 9, 1862; at the naval battle of Drewry's Bluff, May 15, 1862; at Charleston, S. C., during 1863; at the capture of the United States gunboat at Newbern February 4, 1864; at the capture of Plymouth, N. C., on the cruiser Tallahassee; and surrendered with the naval brigade under Raphael Semmes at Appomattox. Daniel was a jovial, lovely boy, and his comrades will shed a tear when they hear that he has crossed the river.

[W. F. Clayton, Florence, S. C., January 9, 1917.]

DR. J. D. WAGNER.

Dr. James D. Wagner, pioneer physician of Selma, Cal., died at Long Beach on October 15, 1916. He was born in Savannah, Tenn., in October, 1844, and his boyhood days were spent on a farm, but his youthful inclinations were to practice medicine. He enlisted in the Southern cause when but sixteen years of age, fought under Gen. Joseph E. Johnston in the Army of Tennessee, and also served as a member of Company G, 1st Tennessee Cavalry, under Gen. Joseph Wheeler. He narrowly escaped being buried alive in the battle of New Hope Church when a shell struck the tree behind which he was fighting, felling him to the ground. Thinking him dead, his comrades wrapped him in a blanket for burial, when they were obliged to retreat. On recovering consciousness he returned to them alone.

After the war young Wagner went back to the farm, but continued his medical studies, diligently working at his books between school terms, and graduated from the University of Nashville in 1873. He went to California in 1881 and became one of the foremost factors in building up the town of Selma. His practice carried him into the mountains and the country of that section, and he never refused to brave a midnight storm in behalf of those unable to pay him, often providing a sick family with necessities out of his own means.

Dr. Wagner was married in 1869 to Miss Sarah Elizabeth Gray, and to them nine children were born. His wife died in 1886, and in 1896 he married Miss Emma Corbley, who survives him with two daughters and a son of the first marriage.

Dr. Wagner was prominent in the social life of Selma and in its Church work, being a charter member and an officer of the Methodist Episcopal Church. He was also a charter member of the Masonic Lodge there, which he served in different offices, and was an officer in the Chapter of the Royal Arcanum. He was always active in community affairs, serving on the school and city boards at different times, and took a leading part in county and State politics. He was a member of the Sterling Price Camp, U. C. V., of Fresno County, and was interested in all its work.

Col. A. C. McAlister.

After an illness of several months, Col. A. C. McAlister, one of the oldest and most substantial citizens of Ashboro, N. C., answered the last roll call on December 8, 1916. He had entered upon his seventy-ninth year. His example and influence will be long felt in the community in which he lived. Colonel McAlister was educated at the University of North Carolina, graduating in the class of 1858. He entered the service of the Confederate States early in the war and rose to the rank of colonel by his gallantry and efficient service. He commanded his regiment, the 46th North Carolina Infantry, in a number of the most serious engagements and always so as to deserve the commendation of his superior officers.

After the war Colonel McAlister lived for a few years in Alamance County, which he represented in the legislature during the Reconstruction period. It is a matter of history that he was especially detailed and served the writ of habeas corpus upon the notorious Kirk, who had terrorized the central part of the State. Later he moved to Randolph County and took part in its politics, for many years being the efficient chairman of the Democratic Committee and winning many hard-fought battles. He was for thirty years an elder in the Presbyterian Church, and at the time of his death he was chairman of the School Board of Ashboro, which position he had held for several years. His last public service was rendered as director of the State Board of Public Charities.

Colonel McAlister is survived by his wife, four sons, and two daughters. Many friends and admirers were present at the last sad rites to this courteous, kindly gentleman, who was loved for his Christian integrity, culture of mind, gentleness of heart, and the all-embracing charity and nobility of his soul.

Members of Camp at Hernando, Miss.

Commander W. L. Glenn, of De Soto Camp, No. 220, U. C. V., at Hernando, Miss., sends a list of losses in membership during 1916 and says: "We are rapidly passing away, and in a few more years the last Confederate will have gone to his reward."

Alfred Dockery, captain Company E, 38th North Carolina Infantry; W. J. Bynum, Company A, 7th Tennessee Cavalry; J. H. Crumpler, Company A, 10th Mississippi Infantry; J. M. Coggins, Crozier's Mississippi Artillery; T. A. Dunn, Company I, 29th Mississippi Infantry; Francis Holmes, lieutenant Company I, 29th Mississippi Infantry; H. N. Harbin, Company F, 42d Mississippi Infantry; W. H. Love, Hart's Battalion of Alabama Infantry; J. T. Malone, Company I, 29th Mississippi Infantry; R. P. Bogan, Company I, 10th Mississippi Infantry; E. H. Randall, Company A, 7th Tennessee Cavalry; G. W. Dixon, Company F, 18th Mississippi Cavalry; J. A. Burrus, Company F, 42d Mississippi Infantry.

Deaths in J. E. B. Stuart Camp, of Terrell, Tex.

Vic Reinhardt, Adjutant, reports the losses in J. E. B. Stuart Camp, No. 45, U. C. V., Terrell, Tex., for 1916:

P. G. Nebhut, captain Company H, 14th Texas Infantry.

James T. Rowell, private Company D, 41st Tennessee Infantry.

W. L. Camp, private Company K, 27th Louisiana Infantry.

McD. Kerby, first lieutenant Company I, 11th Tennessee Cavalry.

H. C. Graves, private Company I, 43d Tennessee Infantry.

J. H. Graham, private Company I, 12th Kentucky Cavalry.

Joseph Mason Kern.

Joseph Mason Kern was born at Romney, Va. (now West Virginia), July 9, 1842, and died in Brevard, N. C., September 5, 1916. At seventeen years of age he enlisted in the Hampshire Guards, a volunteer company of Romney. The following year this company was ordered to Harper's Ferry and became a part of the 13th Virginia Infantry, Col. A. P. Hill. On July 18, with other organizations under the command of Gen. Joseph E. Johnston, the regiment moved to join General Beauregard at Manassas. In entraining at Piedmont Station the regiment became divided, only half of it reaching Manassas with the rest of the brigade in time to assist in the battle. After wintering at Centerville, Va., the regiment did picket duty for some time at Mason's Hills, seven miles from Washington and in sight of the Capitol's dome. In the spring of 1862 the division was sent to join Gen. T. J. Jackson, took part in the celebrated Valley Campaign, then moved to Richmond to join General Lee.

At Cold Harbor Comrade Kern was wounded in the leg, and while recovering he was given a clerkship in the Treasury Department, C. S. A. In March, 1863, he resigned and, his wound still incapacitating him from infantry duty, enlisted in the cavalry, Company D, 11th Virginia. He was captured a few weeks later and sent to Camp Chase, Ohio. Later he was transferred to Johnson's Island Prison and there held five months. From thence, with other prisoners to the number of two thousand five hundred, he was sent to the prison camp at Point Lookout, Md. He was exchanged and sent to Richmond February 22, 1865, after nearly twenty-two months of prison life.

In the fall of 1865 Comrade Kern moved to Mississippi, living twenty years in Natchez and five years in Jackson. At Natchez he was Adjutant of the local Camp, U. C. V., for several years. In 1908 he moved to Brevard, N. C., where for some years, or until age and infirmity rendered it impossible, he was Adjutant of that Camp. He was a regular attendant at all of the Confederate Reunions.

In 1868 Mr. Kern married Miss Jane Sivley, of Raymond, Miss., who died in 1900. He is survived by two daughters, Miss Florence Kern and Mrs. Harold Vernor Smedberg, both of Brevard.

Capt. S. E. Kierolf.

Capt. S. E. Kierolf, who died at the home of his daughter, Mrs. R. D. Dodson, near Alamo, Tenn., on July 11, 1916, was born in New York City November 2, 1833. His father was Jacob Elias Kierolf, from Norway, and his mother, Juliet De Bretton, was a Dane, both of the nobility. With their infant son they went to Mississippi and from there to Madison, Tenn., where the boy was reared to manhood. When young Kierolf was about twenty-three years of age he went to West Tennessee, where he married Miss Mary Harris, and they journeyed happily together through fifty-seven years of married life. He entered the service of the Confederacy at the beginning of the war, joining the company raised in his community, and at the organization of the regiment, the 27th Tennessee, he was made quartermaster. He was captured near Lexington, Tenn., with Col. Alex Campbell and Major Clark, of Jackson, Tenn., by General Hatch and sent to Johnson Island Prison for two years. Some humorous incidents of that prison life are given in the article published in the VETERAN for December, 1916, page 555, which was sent to the VETERAN shortly before his death.

DR. EUGENE LANIER DEADERICK.

Dr. Eugene L. Deaderick was born at Jonesboro, Tenn., August 16, 1843. He was educated in the schools of that town and at the East Tennessee University, now the University of Tennessee, at Knoxville. Early in the War between the States he volunteered as a soldier in the Confederate army, serving faithfully until the close of hostilities, in 1865. He then devoted himself to the study of medicine and received the degree of M.D. at the Jefferson Medical College, in Philadelphia, Pa. He became a successful physician, having practiced his profession in Jonesboro, Knoxville, and Johnson City. He was married to Miss Rebekah Williams, of North Carolina, and seven children were born to them, but none of them survived him; his wife too died several years ago, leaving him entirely without a family of his own. Besides the sorrow of being bereaved of his dear ones, Dr. Deaderick suffered greatly from physical ailments during the latter part of his life, and death was welcomed as a relief from all his sorrows and sufferings. His faith was strong, and he was ready when the summons came on December 4, 1916.

Dr. Deaderick was a man of modest and gentle demeanor, but at the same time firm in his convictions of right and duty. A friend said of him: "If we were all like Dr. Deaderick, there would be no need of courts and laws." Kind and considerate of the rights of others, he seemed to desire to practice the Golden Rule in all his dealings with his fellow man.

DR. THOMAS PROCTOR.

Dr. Thomas Proctor, who died at Monroe City, Mo., on December 12, 1916, was born near Philadelphia, in Marion County, Mo., on May 26, 1839. Upon the breaking out of the War between the States he entered the Missouri State Guard under Colonel Green and was with General Price in the battle of Lexington. During the retreat south he was stricken with typhoid fever and left behind. On his recovery, finding that he was north of the Federal lines and being unable to rejoin his command, he entered the Iowa University at Keokuk, graduating from that institution with the degree of M.D. in 1864.

Dr. Proctor practiced medicine at Withers Mill and Monroe City until 1881, when he entered the Monroe City Bank as cashier. In 1887 he became its president and held that position until his death. For many years, up to the time of his death, he served as treasurer of the Monroe City School District and was also treasurer of the First Baptist Church. He was married to Miss Luta Bailey in April, 1865, and is survived by his wife and four sons. His brother, David M. Proctor, also of Monroe City, is the only surviving member of a family of eleven.

The life of Dr. Proctor was one of far-reaching influence. He was a factor in the business, social, educational, and religious life of his community, and his example will be an inspiration to those who come after him.

DEATHS IN STOCKDALE CAMP, No. 324, U. C. V.

Commander W. C. Vaught reports the following losses in membership of Stockdale Camp, No. 324, U. C. V., at Magnolia, Miss., within the past twelve months:

H. S. Brumfield, S. C. Walker, and Edward Pierce, 38th Mississippi Infantry; H. A. Dawson, 45th Mississippi Infantry; Thomas Lard, 7th Mississippi Infantry; W. L. Scott, 33d Mississippi Infantry; J. W. Lyles, 9th Louisiana Infantry.

JOHN HARVEY ARTHUR.

John Harvey Arthur died at his home, in Arthur City, Lamar County, Tex., October 30, 1916. He was born in Tennessee August 31, 1824, and moved to Georgia with his parents when quite young. On reaching maturity he engaged in merchandizing in Calhoun, Ga. In March, 1862, young Arthur enlisted in Company E, 40th Georgia Regiment, Barton's Brigade, under Capt. J. F. Groover and Col. Abney Johnson. At Perryville, in October, 1862, he was captured by the Federals and sent to Louisville, Ky., and later to Vicksburg, Miss. He was exchanged in February, 1863.

After the war Mr. Arthur resumed merchandizing at Calhoun, Ga. He was county treasurer for eight years; then moved to Lamar County, Tex., and engaged in merchandizing and cotton-planting at what is now Arthur City until his death.

He was married in November, 1868, to Miss Sue Lane, of a Georgia family, and to them a son and daughter were born. His son died in 1914 and his wife in 1916, leaving only the daughter, now the wife of C. D. Purdon, chief engineer of the St. Louis and Southwestern Railway lines.

J. J. ESTES.

J. J. Estes was born in Kanawha County (now Putnam County, W. Va.) on the 30th of March, 1838, and died December 19, 1916, after a lingering illness of more than two years, and was buried by the side of his wife. He was a gallant Confederate soldier, having joined Capt. W. R. Gunn's company, D, 8th Virginia Cavalry, in August, 1862. He was captured in 1864 and remained a prisoner in Camp Chase, Ohio, until the close of the war.

He was a member of Camp Garnett, No. 902, U. C. V., of Huntington, W. Va., and was held in high esteem by his comrades; was also a member of Mount Vernon Baptist Church, near his home, for about fifty years.

Resolved, That, while we shall miss him from our meetings, we realize that our loss is his gain, for we trust that he has entered into rest "where sickness, sorrow, pain, and death are felt and feared no more."

[Committee: C. A. Reece, N. C. Petit, M. McClung.]

GEORGE J. HOLLEY.

George Jeff Holley, born in South Carolina in 1839, enlisted in the Confederate army in Louisiana as a member of Company B, 9th Missouri Cavalry. He served faithfully during the hard campaigning of his command and remained till the last battle was fought and the surrender came at Appomattox. He was a member of Cunningham Camp, U. C. V., at Kemp, Tex., and was always glad to meet with his comrades. He went to Texas in 1866 and was there married to Miss Martha Jackson in 1869. He reared a large family, all of whom occupy positions of usefulness. His death occurred at Kemp, at the home of his daughter, on October 19, 1916, after many years of suffering. His oldest son, Rev. Edgar Holley, is a Methodist minister of prominence and ability and is now a student at Chicago University.

DENNIS DUGAN.—Dennis Dugan, who died at Galesburg, Ill., in November, 1916, served in the Confederate army as one of the Louisiana Tigers and was severely wounded in the battle of Antietam. He had accumulated quite a fortune during his lifetime, in addition to which, it is said, he was drawing a pension from the State of Louisiana and also from the Santa Fe Railroad.

J. L. ROBERSON.

J. L. Roberson enlisted from Chickasaw County, Miss., in the spring of 1861, joining Company H, 11th Mississippi Regiment, and served with General Lee in the Virginia Army. He was at Cold Harbor, Seven Pines, and Gettysburg; was captured near Richmond just before the surrender and kept in prison until the last of June, 1865. He was born July 14, 1837, and died November 25, 1916, at Wynne, Ark. He removed from Mississippi to Arkansas in 1885. Only a short time before his death he had celebrated his golden wedding anniversary. His wife and four sons survive him. Comrade Roberson was a member of Marion Cogbill Camp, No. 1316, U. C. V., and loved to meet with his comrades of the sixties. He was a man of kindly disposition and loved by all who knew him. W. P. BREWER.

J. L. ROBERSON.

DEATHS IN CAMP AT TALLADEGA, ALA.

The committee from Camp No. 246, U. C. V., of Talladega, Ala., reports the death of two members in November, 1916:

G. K. Miller, born in Talladega in December, 1836, was the first white child born in that town. He entered the Confederate service in July, 1861, and remained until the war closed. A brave and faithful soldier, he was also an honest and upright citizen and a true and consistent member of the Presbyterian Church. The Camp has lost a worthy member, the community a worthy and useful citizen.

J. K. Jones, born April 20, 1845, entered the Confederate army in March, 1862, as a private of Company K, 30th Alabama Regiment, and remained in service to the close of the war. He made a gallant soldier and was none the less faithful to the duties of civil and religious life. His loss was deeply felt in the community, and his place in Camp and Church cannot be filled.

THOMAS A. GILL.

After a lingering illness, Thomas Allison Gill died at the home of his nephew, E. W. Gill, near Whon, Tex., on November 15, 1916. He was born in Green County, Ala., February 14, 1837, and went with his parents to Arkansas in 1843. At the beginning of the War between the States he enlisted in Capt. Joe Neal's company at Marshall, Ark., and was sent to the northern part of the State to Col. Tom P. Dockery's regiment, which was soon disbanded. He then joined the 19th Arkansas early in 1862 and was sent to General Pike at Fort McCulloch; was removed from there in June and served the remainder of the war in General Price's command, following him in his raid through Missouri. When the regiment was disbanded in June, 1865, he returned to his home, in Arkansas, and removed to Ellis County, Tex., in 1871.

Comrade Gill was never married and spent the latter part of his life with the family of his brother, the late J. M. Gill. He was a member of the Methodist Church and lived a true Christian life. Of the family of two brothers and four sisters, only a sister is left, Mrs. M. J. Patterson, of Childress, Tex.

WILLIAM ANDREW GRIFFIN.

In Oakdale, Stanislaus County, Cal., on December 24, 1916, the spirit of that brave soldier and Christian gentleman, William Andrew Griffin, went to the God who gave it. The Oakdale *Leader* referred to him as "a man of keen intellect, a close student of public affairs, and one who lived his life bravely, as he had fought for his country."

William A. Griffin was born in Monroe, Walton County, Ga., October 4, 1836, going when a young man to Augusta. When the War between the States began he enlisted in the Oglethorpe Infantry, which left Augusta on April 1, 1861, for Macon, where it was mustered in as a company of the 1st Georgia Regiment of Volunteers, C. S. A., under Col. James N. Ramsey, of Columbus, Ga. The regiment went to Pensacola, Fla., and there saw service for several months. In June, 1861, it was ordered to Virginia and took an active part in the West Virginia campaign. In March, 1862, the regiment was sent to Augusta, Ga., and mustered out, being a twelve months' regiment. In April young Griffin reënlisted for the war in the Oglethorpe Infantry, Company B, commanded by his cousin, Capt. Ewin W. Ansley, who was killed in the battle of Murfreesboro, Tenn., December 31, 1862. The company went to Corinth, Miss., in April, 1862, being assigned to the 5th Georgia Regiment of Volunteers and later incorporated as Company C in the 2d Georgia Battalion of Sharpshooters, Jackson's Brigade.

In 1863 Comrade Griffin was made orderly (first) sergeant of the company and was serving as such when he received a desperate wound in front of Atlanta July 31, 1864, his right elbow being shattered. He took part in the fighting in Kentucky, also at Murfreesboro, Chickamauga, Missionary Ridge, and was in all the engagements of his command from Dalton to Atlanta, Ga., until disabled for further service. As a soldier he was brave and faithful, as a friend true and steadfast, and as a Christian pure. Only some six or seven of those who belonged to Company C from April, 1862, to April, 1865, are now living. Comrade Griffin is survived by his wife, two daughters, and a son.

[A tribute of love to "dear Grif" from his comrade and friend, Frank Stovall Roberts, Company C, 2d Georgia Battalion of Sharpshooters.]

CAIN BATES.

Comrade Abel Bates, of Mansfield, La., reports the death of his twin brother, Cain Bates, on October 4, 1916, at the age of seventy-one years. They served in the same company of the 44th Battalion of Virginia Volunteers, of Petersburg, from the latter part of 1863, and two other brothers, Tom and Nat, were also in the Confederate army. Tom Bates passed away about two years ago in the Soldiers' Home in Richmond, Va., and Nat died several years ago at his home, near Como, Miss. They belonged to Pickett's Division, and both were wounded in the battle of Gettysburg. The oldest brother, Bob, died in Richmond during the war. All were born in Halifax County, Va. Two brothers, Abel and Dave, survive. Cain Bates died at Homer, La.

HEALY-CLAYBROOK CAMP, U. C. V.

Dr. D. B. Dutton, of Lol, Va., reports the following deaths among the members of Healy-Claybrook Camp, No. 57, U. C. V., during the past year: Adjutant John Hardy, Warren Carter, R. D. Hilliard, Zadoe Clayville, Elisha Clayville, and Ephraim Young. Mr. Young was one of the crew on the Virginia (Merrimac) in her famous fight with the Monitor in Hampton Roads.

United Daughters of the Confederacy

MRS. CORDELIA POWELL ODENHEIMER, *President General*

Washington, D. C.

MRS. J. H. STEWART, Los Angeles, Cal..........*First Vice President General*	MRS. R. E. LITTLE, Wadesboro, N. C.......................*Treasurer General*
MRS. L. M. BASHINSKY, Troy, Ala............*Second Vice President General*	MRS. S. E. F. ROSE, West Point, Miss......................*Historian General*
MRS. LULU A. LOVELL, Denver, Colo..........*Third Vice President General*	MRS. J. NORMENT POWELL, Johnson City, Tenn............*Registrar General*
MRS. W. C. N. MERCHANT, Chatham, Va........*Recording Secretary General*	MRS. E. T. SELLS, Columbus, Ohio.....................*Custodian of Crosses*
MRS. LUTIE HAILEY WALCOTT, Ardmore, Okla........*Cor. Secretary General*	MRS. FRANK ANTHONY WALKE, Norfolk, Va..*Custodian Flags and Pennants*

MRS. A. A. CAMPBELL, Wytheville, Va., *Official Editor.*

"Love Makes Memory Eternal"

FROM THE PRESIDENT GENERAL.

Dear Daughters: February seems late to acknowledge the many loving Christmas and New Year greetings you sent me, but I want you to know how deeply I prize them. The apparent delay is due to my communications having necessarily to reach the VETERAN a month before you read them.

Please do not think that I am neglectful of you when your letters are not answered immediately. I receive many each day, some of them requiring careful consideration and the most urgent demanding the earliest reply. During November and December the greater portion of my time was taken up in forming committees and communicating with our general officers, that the machinery of the society be put in order for the year's work; but I endeavor to answer every communication as promptly as possible.

The first thing I want to draw your attention to is the audit of the report of our former Treasurer General, Mrs. C. B. Tate. I know that every one of you has a full realization and appreciation of the seven years of faithful and conscientious service she gave us, and it is with a feeling of pride that I quote the remark of the auditor: "The first glance at her books showed me how little trouble I would have, as they were so systematically kept." The correctness of this assertion was affirmed in his subsequent indorsement: "Every disbursement was supported by proper evidence of payment and duly authorized by proper authority." Mrs. Tate fully realized that when a society had grown to the size ours has attained strictly business methods must be used to conduct it.

Sir Moses Ezekiel sent you through me his Christmas and New Year's greeting.

Miss Gautreaux has just written me that she has forwarded Louisiana's final pledge of $135 for Arlington to Mrs. Little, Treasurer General, and I trust that many others have sent in theirs. While it was a task to raise the required sum, I am confident, Daughters, that we will never regret the time and effort expended upon this magnificent monument.

In a recent letter from Mrs. Trader she states that she is improving, but must stay at the hospital longer to insure a complete cure of her malady. It was a bitter disappointment to her to learn that, after her hopes had been aroused by an error in the newspapers, the resolution by the late Mrs. Van Wyck, read by Mrs. C. C. Clay, of California, urging that one hundred dollars a month be given to her, was not acted upon by the convention. Pledges were made and a small amount given from the floor, but not enough to insure the barest existence. Therefore, Daughters, let me again urge you to remember your pledges made at the Washington convention in 1912.

I hope next month to give you the exact amount yet to be collected for the payment of the window to the Confederate women of the sixties to be placed in the Red Cross Building.

When the Veterans, Sons, and Southern Memorial Association meet in Washington in June, we wish to unveil this window, and to do so it must be paid for in full.

When Gen. Bennett H. Young, former Commander of the United Confederate Veterans, so eloquently told us at Dallas of the great shaft it was planned to erect in memory of Jefferson Davis at his old home, Fairview, Ky., and urged our assistance, we heartily indorsed this memorial, but made no definite pledges. I have appointed directors of committees representing each State, and from what I know of the women composing them I am confident that material help will be given.

On December 7 I attended the annual convention of the District of Columbia Division, at which I addressed the delegates, and on December 8 I went to Baltimore for the annual meeting of the Maryland Division. During the week of December 11 I was the guest of Mrs. Frank Anthony Walke in Norfolk, Va., where I represented you at the Southern Commercial Congress. While there I attended many brilliant functions, receiving at all, among them being the reception given by the Norfolk Woman's Auxiliary, Miss Nannie Kensett, Chairman, at the Monticello Hotel; luncheon by Miss Serpell, State Regent, D. A. R.; reception at the home of Mrs. Wilke given by the Hope Maury Chapter, U. D. C., and the Pickett-Buchanan Chapter, U. D. C.; luncheon in honor of Mrs. Julian Heath at Southland Hotel by the National Housewives' League; reception by the members of the Virginia Club; reception by Admiral and Mrs. Walter McLean at the Navy Yard; reception by the Great Bridge Chapter, D. A. R.; reception by the Women's Club; and a trip on the steamer Memphis to review the battleships off Old Point. The Presidents General of our sister societies were present during the Congress, and I had the pleasure also of meeting many members of our own organization.

On New Year's Day I attended an eggnog luncheon given by Miss Frances Washington Weeks at her home, in Washington, in honor of Camp 171, United Confederate Veterans, and on New Year's night I received with Mrs. James Mulcare, the newly elected President, Miss Mary Custis Lee, and the Division officers at the reception given in honor of the Confederate Veterans by the District of Columbia Division at the Confederate Memorial Home.

An important part of our work for the year 1917 should be in the interest of a more general circulation of the CONFEDERATE VETERAN among the members of this organization. As our official organ, the columns of the VETERAN are always open to the Daughters of the Confederacy, furnishing such a means of communication between Divisions and Chapters and for exploiting our work as could be gotten in no other way so effectively, and for this there is no expense to the organization. All that is asked is that the membership through individual and Chapter subscriptions get the benefit of what is published. When we consider that other patriotic organizations support their official organs by a heavy tax on the general treasury, we can realize that little is being asked of us while much is being given.

Take this thought to heart, my dear Daughters, and let us make this year (1917) the banner year in the life of the VET-ERAN. With the rapid thinning of the ranks of the Confederate veterans, there is consequent decrease in the subscription patronage of this publication, and we must see that the loss is made up in the ranks of the Daughters and Sons. In the support we give it will we show our appreciation of the bequest by its founder. Send to the office at Nashville for sample copies and subscription offers.

Faithfully yours,   CORDELIA POWELL ODENHEIMER,
President General.

SUBSCRIPTIONS FOR PRINTING LAST ADDRESS OF MISS RUTHERFORD, HISTORIAN GENERAL U. D. C., 1911-16.

THE CIVILIZATION OF THE OLD SOUTH.

DALLAS, TEX., November 9, 1916.
When Mrs. Williams, Recording Secretary General, announced that there would not be a sufficient amount of money in the U. D. C. treasury to print her minutes and Miss Rutherford's address also, volunteer offerings were suggested after a motion was made that the address must be printed. These offerings came so rapidly that when a sufficient amount was thought to be in hand the President General and the Recording Secretary General called a halt, while yet a long line stood eager to give. By a motion of Mrs. Eakins these subscriptions were to be sent direct to Miss Rutherford to be used as she desired in her historical work.

Mrs. Odenheimer, the President General, notified Miss Rutherford that she would request Mrs. Little, the Treasurer General, to forward the list of subscribers to her at once in order that she make the collections and use them as by Mrs. Eakins's suggestion.

The list as sent by Mrs. Williams shows only $592 promised, while the announcement was made from the platform when the halt was called that $612 had been recorded, and later some supplemental gifts raised the amount to $630.

Many of the recorded gifts are lacking in complete address; so the list is printed at Miss Rutherford's request, that the names and amounts accidentally omitted and others added may be sent to her at once.

Owing to the expense of printing this year, the amount recorded below will not be sufficient to print and distribute the twenty thousand copies ordered, and the order for printing was made on the promise of a cash payment; so any supplemental gifts will be appreciated and can be added to the list of collections reported next month.

It was the thought of the subscribers that the amount would also be sufficient to secure stronger binders for the fifty-five volumes of history prepared by Miss Rutherford to be placed in the Confederate Museum at Richmond. The present binders are considered inadequate to properly protect the valuable material, as Miss Rutherford stated in her historical report.

All checks are requested to be made payable to ex-Historian General U. D. C. and sent to Miss Mildred Rutherford, Athens, Ga.

Mrs Emma H. Townsend, Corsicana, Tex.....	$ 10 00
C. S. A. Chapter, Dallas, Tex...............	100 00
S. A. Gerrald, a veteran.........................	10 00
Ohio Division (paid)............................	20 00
California Division (paid)........................	25 00
Arkansas Division...............................	25 00
Mrs. C. L. Randle, Kentucky (paid)...............	10 00
Mrs. S. M. Ward, Kentucky.......................	5 00
William B. Bate Chapter, Nashville, Tenn..........	5 00
Nashville Chapter, No. 1.........................	5 00
Harriet Overton Chapter, Nashville...............	10 00
T. M. Wall.....................................	10 00
Texas Division.................................	25 00
Mrs Cornelia Branch Stone (paid).................	5 00
North Carolina Division.........................	25 00
Bessemer Chapter, Alabama.......................	5 00
Mrs. Peter Youree, Louisiana (paid)..............	50 00
Georgia Division................................	10 00
Georgia Children of the Confederacy..............	5 00
Baltimore Chapter (paid)........................	15 00
Maryland Division..............................	10 00
Missouri Chapter...............................	5 00
Sarah Law Chapter, Memphis, Tenn. (paid)........	10 00
Hood Texas Brigade, Junior C. of C..............	5 00
Virginia Division...............................	30 00
Dallas Chapter, Dallas, Tex......................	25 00
Philadelphia Chapter (paid).....................	10 00
Mary Mildred Sullivan Chapter, New York..........	10 00
William R. Scury Chapter, Texas..................	5 00
Barnard E. Bee Chapter, San Antonio.............	5 00
Mary West Chapter, Waco, Tex....................	5 00
O. C. Horn Chapter.............................	5 00
Stonewall Band, C. of C., New Orleans............	5 00
Hannibal Boone Chapter.........................	5 00
Frank Bennett C. of C., Wadesboro, N. C..........	2 00
Mrs. Bannermann, Louisiana (paid)...............	5 00
J. J. Finley Chapter, Gainesville, Fla. (paid)......	5 00
Mrs. Charles E. Parr............................	5 00
Julia Jackson Chapter, Fort Worth................	5 00
Winnie Davis Chapter............................	5 00
Monroe Chapter, North Carolina..................	5 00
Mrs. R. V. Houston, Monroe, N. C................	5 00
Atoka, Okla., C. of C............................	5 00
Oklahoma C. of C. (paid)........................	5 00
Children of the Confederacy, Tulsa, Okla. (paid)....	5 00
Cash	30 00
Total	$592 00

Check received from Mrs. Little, Treasurer General U. D. C., December 30, 1916, $175.

THE BOOK COMMITTEE, U. D. C.

Miss Mildred Rutherford has been appointed Chairman of the Southern Literature Committee, U. D. C., and through the VETERAN she asks authors of books relating to the South to send them to her for examination, so that recommendation may be given to those true to the South and her ideals. She also asks that these books be considered as gifts to a Confederate library and so autographed, which library will be placed by action of the next convention and added to year by year. As soon as the committee is complete the names will be sent for publication, so that each State chairman can do her part in commending or rejecting books.

THE MISSISSIPPI DIVISION.

BY MRS. CORA M. DU BOSE, CHARLESTON, MISS.

Inasmuch as the Mississippi Division presented the name of one of her gifted members as Historian General, the convention, U. D. C., held at Dallas, Tex., in November, was of special interest to Mississippi Daughters. Mrs. Rose's name was received without opposition and amid much applause. She is recognized as a woman of wonderful personality and rare executive ability, serving her Division ably as Historian and President, and as the author of "The Ku-Klux Klan" is known as a writer of ability. The Division is justly proud of the high honor accorded her, but feels that it is deserved.

The Daughters of the Mississippi Division have been untiring in their support of Arlington and Shiloh and have at last been rewarded for their efforts. Since these monuments have been paid for, attention can be turned toward the memorial window to be placed in the Red Cross Building at the nation's capital as a tribute of love and honor to those noble mothers, wives, and sweethearts who bravely endured all the hardships of the War between the States. Congress has honored itself by honoring the women of the sixties and in so doing has brought forth the love and admiration of the solid South.

The Mississippi Division is wide awake to all things pertaining to the good of the work and is progressing surely toward its goal under the brilliant leadership of its gifted president, Mrs. Virginia Redditt Price, of Carrollton.

Many new Chapters have been organized during the last few months. New energy has been infused into the work, and all loyal Daughters are determined to make the year of 1917 a banner year in history.

THE SOUTH CAROLINA DIVISION.

BY MRS. LOUISE AYER VANDIVER.

South Carolina Chapters have accomplished good work in various lines. At the State convention, which met in Union in November, 1916, Mrs. McWhirter, Division President, presented to Dick Anderson Chapter, of Sumter, the South Carolina banner for greatest increase in membership. Miss Bertie Smith, Vice President of the Piedmont District, presented three gavels to Chapters in her district for most excellent work, one going to Calvin Crozier Chapter, of Newberry, for the greatest disbursement of money for U. D. C. work during the year. This Chapter gave over $200 for educational purposes alone and gained the State banner as well as the District gavel. Miss Smith presented a gavel to the William Wallace Chapter, of Union, for gaining the greatest number of new members of any Chapter in the District for the year, and she gave one to Hampton-Lee Chapter, of Greer, for the best all-round work of the year.

At Thanksgiving the Cheraw Chapter made glad the hearts of a number of needy veterans by generous gifts of groceries. The Mary Ann Bowie Chapter, of Johnston, following its yearly custom, served a bountiful Thanksgiving dinner to the inmates of its County Home.

The Edgefield Chapter and Robert E. Lee Chapter, of Anderson, sent, as usual, generous gifts, prettily arranged, to their County Homes at Christmas, and the old people in these institutions look forward to this Santa Claus visit with as much eagerness as the little ones anticipate the yearly visit of the same old saint.

In the U. D. C. department of The State Mrs. McWhirter has a Christmas letter of greeting and encouragement to her numerous Daughters, and she urges them especially to put forth every effort to gain new members during the coming year, that South Carolina's vote may be large for the candidate for President whom she expects to present to the next general convention.

General Reed, South Carolina's commanding officer of Confederate Veterans, has asked the Chapters of the State to assist in providing Confederate uniforms for veterans who cannot get them for themselves, to be worn at State and general reunions and all other Confederate gatherings which they may attend and to serve these faithful sons of Dixie as burial robes, feeling that perhaps their last long sleep may be sweeter if the worn old frame is laid to rest in Confederate gray. Many of the Chapters have taken up the work.

Dick Anderson Chapter, of Sumter, has offered ten prizes to county schools for the best celebration of Lee's birthday.

Several Chapters are making special efforts to collect and preserve personal recollections of the war as told by veterans. It was in collecting these reminiscences that the Mary Ann Bowie Chapter, of Johnston, made its wonderful record last year, fifty-two papers being handed to the State Historian, thus winning for South Carolina the historical banner.

THE OHIO DIVISION.

BY MRS. ANNE D. WEST, CINCINNATI.

The annual convention of the Ohio Division, U. D. C., was held in Dayton October 10-12, 1916, the hostess Chapter being the Gen. Joe Wheeler Chapter of Dayton, Mrs. E. H. Estabrook, President. Mrs. Elizabeth T. Sells, State President, conducted the convention with her usual tact and executive ability. All six Chapters of the State had delegates, and the Chapter Presidents' reports were full of interest. All Chapters have given largely to needy veterans, women of the Confederacy, scholarships, and the General Relief Fund. Emphasis was laid on the need of a State educational fund, and this was left in the hands of an able committee.

A beautiful memorial service was held in memory of those lately deceased. The convention came to a close after much business had been accomplished, and thanks were given to the hostess Chapter for a delightful time socially.

DAUGHTERS IN PENNSYLVANIA.

The Pittsburgh Chapter, No. 1605, U. D. C., made a plea for truthful statements in Southern history at its annual historical meeting on December 15, 1916, in the William Penn Hotel, Pittsburgh. Mrs. Fannie L. Hoof, Chapter Historian, read Miss Mildred Rutherford's address on "The South in the Building of the Nation," and Mrs. J. Marvin Hall read the essay on "The Confederate Private," which won the prize offered by Hope Maury Chapter, of Norfolk, Va. A musical program followed.

Mrs. John Pryor Cowan, President of the Chapter, and Mrs. J. Marvin Hall, Registrar, attended on December 12 a meeting for the observance of the one hundred and twenty-ninth anniversary of the Statehood of Pennsylvania as guests of the Women's Relief Corps, Nos. 1 and 60, of the Grand Army of the Republic.

Historical Department, U. D. C.

Motto: "Loyalty to the truth of Confederate history."
Key word: "Preparedness." Flower: The Rose.

MRS. S. E. F. ROSE, HISTORIAN GENERAL U. D. C.

The Historic Yearbooks for 1917 have been distributed, and all is in readiness for the Chapters to begin the year's study. The programs give events in chronological order, thus forming a great chain, and you cannot afford to miss a single link. Your Historian is deeply grateful for so many complimentary letters as to the plan of study and feels more than repaid already for the time and study spent in the preparation of the programs. The notes will be brief this month, as the U. D. C. and C. of C. programs for February and March are being placed in this number, so as to restore the regular order of having programs appear in advance. Read every word in the Yearbook, as all necessary information is contained therein, and thus undue correspondence may be avoided. Study the historical contests and prepare to enter one of them, and have the children study programs arranged for them. The form of opening meetings, whether by ritual or prayer, is left to the preference of each Chapter, also as to selections for music and readings, however the suggestion being offered that selections be from our Southern authors. Remember the motto and keyword of the Historical Department and let every month's study be such as will count in the final reckoning of the historical work for 1917.

MRS. S. E. F. ROSE.

U. D. C. PROGRAM FOR FEBRUARY, 1917.

TOPICS FOR FEBRUARY PAPERS.

Events of 1861: Secession of Florida, January 10; Alabama, January 11; Georgia, January 19; Louisiana, January 26; Texas, February 10.

Tell of the organization of the Confederate States government, February 4, at Montgomery, Ala., first capital of the Southern Confederacy, by the seven seceded States. Personnel of first Confederate Cabinet. Inauguration of Jefferson Davis, President, and Alexander H. Stephens, Vice President, Confederate States of America, February 18.

Who were the peace commissioners sent by Jefferson Davis to confer with the Federal government, and what was the result?

Describe the first Confederate flag. When, where, and by whom was it raised?

Round-table discussion: "Was the South the first to threaten secession, and were the statesmen of the South the only noted statesmen who held that under certain conditions a State had a right to secede?"

U. D. C. PROGRAM FOR MARCH, 1917.

TOPICS FOR MARCH PAPERS.

Events of 1861: Bombardment of Fort Sumter, April 12. Who was the Confederate commander, and who was in command of the fort? Lincoln's call for 75,000 volunteers to coerce the South, April 15, and the proclamation of blockade of the entire Southern coast. Virginia seceded April 17. Baltimore riot April 19, where the first blood of the war was shed. Tell of this conflict. Arkansas seceded May 6; North Carolina, May 20; Tennessee, June 8, uniting with the Confederacy. Confederate capital moved to Richmond, Va., in May, 1861. Tell of the first meeting of the Confederate Congress there.

Round-table discussion: "Was the firing on Fort Sumter by the Confederates or reënforcements sent to the fort by the Federal government the beginning of the war?" "Was faith as to Sumter fully kept?" "Why was it expedient to move the capital from Montgomery to Richmond?

C. OF C. PROGRAM FOR FEBRUARY, 1917.

What State called the Peace Convention of 1861?

Where was Jefferson Davis when his State, Mississippi, seceded, and what did he do?

Where was the "Bonnie Blue Flag" first sung, and what incident suggested the writing of it, and who was its author?

Where and when was the Southern Confederacy formed?

Who were made President and Vice President of the Confederate States, and when were they inaugurated?

Where was Jefferson Davis when he was elected President of the Confederacy? Did he seek the office?

Who were the peace commissioners sent by him to the Federal government to try to avert the war?

Tell what you know about the first Confederate flag.

"Grandmother's Stories about the War."

Song: "The Bonnie Blue Flag."

Reference, "The South in the Building of the Nation," Volume II.

C. OF C. PROGRAM FOR MARCH, 1917.

Who made the call for 75,000 volunteers to coerce the South back into the Union?

What States seceded in rapid succession after this?

Give dates of their secession and number of States now composing the Southern Confederacy.

Give date of the bombardment of Fort Sumter and where this fort was.

Where was the first blood of the war shed?

What two States passed acts of secession and became Confederate States in October and November, 1861?

What other State attempted to secede?

Were the people living in the Southern States the only ones who owned slaves?

Was not the South trying to free her slaves long before the War between the States?

"Grandfather Stories About the War."

Song, "Maryland, My Maryland."

Reference, "Brief History of the United States," Andrews, Chapter XII.

Confederated Southern Memorial Association

Mrs. W. J. Behan.................................*President*
    New Orleans, La.
Mrs. John E. Maxwell.........................*Treasurer*
    Seale, Ala.
Miss Daisy M. L. Hodgson..........*Recording Secretary*
    7909 Sycamore Street, New Orleans, La.
Miss Mary A. Hall...........................*Historian*
    1106¾ Broad Street, Augusta, Ga.
Mrs. J. Enders Robinson.........*Corresponding Secretary*
    113 Third Street South, Richmond, Va.
Mrs. Virginia Frazer Boyle............*Poet Laureate*
    1015 Union Avenue, Memphis, Tenn.

VICE PRESIDENTS

ALABAMA—Montgomery.....................Mrs. R. P. Dexter
ARKANSAS—Fayetteville ....Mrs. J. Garside Welch
FLORIDA—Pensacola.................Mrs. Horace L. Simpson
GEORGIA—Atlanta....................Mrs. A. McD. Wilson
LOUISIANA—New Orleans..................Mrs. James Dinkins
MISSISSIPPI—Vicksburg ....Mrs. E. C. Carroll
MISSOURI—St. Louis.....................Mrs. G. K. Warner
NORTH CAROLINA—Raleigh...............Mrs. Robert H. Jones
SOUTH CAROLINA—Charleston..........Mrs. S. Cary Beckwith
TENNESSEE—Memphis...............Mrs. Charles W. Frazer
VIRGINIA—Front Royal...............Mrs. S. M. Davis-Roy

Next Convention to be held in Washington, D. C.

MEMORIAL WORK IN ALABAMA.

BY MRS. R. P. DEXTER, VICE PRESIDENT FOR ALABAMA C. S. M. A.

The first day of the new year, 1917, my year's work passes in panoramic view before me, but foremost of all are my memorial duties. Alabama has accomplished much in the past. The question is asked, Are the women of this generation losing interest in the cause their mothers loved so well and for which they labored so unceasingly? No. Last year we celebrated our fiftieth anniversary in perpetuating the memories of the heroes of the sixties, "lest we forget." And the occasion was our grandest success, with the largest crowd and greatest interest manifested. Our work will live and grow, for the women of the Southland will ever pay the debt they owe to the "heroes of yesterday," whose "death is the crowning glory of their lives."

Can we as true, loyal Daughters forget how our mothers, clothed in somber black, the emblem of grief for lost ones, began in '66 to gather dear ones on Alabama soil and place markers? Look on Capitol Hill at the grand monument erected by those heart-bruised mothers to Alabama's dead, to the navy, cavalry, artillery, and infantry. How they struggled and saved! The country was devastated and impoverished in '66; but the Southern woman had learned at her country's shrine the lesson of sacrifice, and shortly the work of wonder and beauty arose. It was a marvel where the accumulated fifty thousand dollars came from; but "earnestness, the key to success," was ever their motto.

Surmounting this shaft is the beautiful Goddess of Peace. When our National Guards were called to mobilize and marched up Dexter Avenue to the Capitol, I thought I saw her hand tremble as though she might draw the sword from its scabbard. This prayer arose in my heart: "God forbid."

President Davis unveiled this beautiful monument, and our mothers said: "The debt is paid." But presently a low phantom voice came from Chickamauga saying: "Don't pass us by. We fell on Kelly's bloody battle field; in the fiercest of the fight fell Alabama's boys." Again these mothers arose, but years had thinned their ranks, and their steps were feeble. "We will begin this work, but, our children, you must finish it." And we did. At the Confederate Veteran Reunion at Chattanooga, Tenn., in 1913 we, the children, unveiled the monument built by the Ladies' Memorial Association of Montgomery, Ala. Scarcely half a dozen of those devoted mothers lived to see the completion of their work. Since the unveiling four have gone to their heavenly home, one of whom was our beloved Vice President of Alabama, Mrs. J. C. Lee. In our pride we did not selfishly take the best site, but left a glorious one for our State monument, which the legislature has promised to erect.

Memorial Day has spread into every city, town, and hamlet in the State. Some say the memorial work has merged into the U. D. C. My friend, you can be a Daughter every day in the year; but if you observe the 26th of April as Memorial Day, then you are for that day a memorial woman and should feel proud of the title. It is the oldest patriotic organization in the South.

The Marion monument ever rises before me, for it is most pathetic, "The Unreturned Dead"—grief without a solace.

The Montgomery Woman's College, with her Junior Memorial and the Mary Graves Lee Junior Memorial, is to the Ladies' Memorial Association its star of hope, for their young, loving hands will carry on our sacred work. The example set by the students of the Alabama Polytechnic Institute is most worthy of emulation by all Southern colleges for our boys.

A letter from Mrs. B. B. Ross, a brilliant, loyal Daughter of Auburn, tells of the beautiful observance of Memorial Day held in that town. Auburn is historic, for in classic Langdon Hall the finest orators of the South have been heard. From Georgia came Seaborn Jones, Alexander Stephens, Ben Hill, and Bob Toombs; among these was our magnificent William L. Yancey. The Auburn students of the days of the sixties, though mere boys, closed their books and nobly responded to their country's call. After a lapse of fifty years Auburn's faculty in 1913 gave to these veterans the diplomas they sacrificed in '61. Auburn students hail from many States in the Union, even from Old Mexico, India, China, and England. The participation in the memorial exercises is not compulsory, but voluntary on the part of the student body. The letter from Mrs. Ross follows:

MEMORIAL DAY IN AUBURN, ALA.

"Memorial Day is indeed a day of days in Auburn's calendar, for beautiful and impressive exercises are annually held in Langdon Hall, where the faculty and the large student body of one thousand splendid young men join the Ladies' Memorial Association, the Daughters of the Confederacy, and the Veterans in paying loving tribute to the matchless heroes of 1861-65.

"The college band, one of the best in the South, is an inspiring addition to a program in which the students take the leading part, a young man from the senior class generally being the orator of the occasion. The commandant of the college is marshal of the day. The students march by companies as the band leads the way to Auburn's cemetery to decorate the soldiers' monument and to place wreaths on the ninety-six graves in the Confederate lot. Songs are sung, a prayer is offered, salutes are fired, and 'Taps' is sounded.

"Memorial Day is observed in answer to the purest dictates

of the heart to teach the truth of history and to keep ever before these splendid young men, the future citizens of our country, the high ideals that acuated their noble Confederate ancestors and to remind them of the devoted and unselfish service their fathers rendered to their State and country.

"So far as known, this is the only Memorial Day observed in connection with a State institution of learning."

One might ask, Does not the annual observance of our Southern patriotic days engender bitterness? No, not at all, for our Confederate veterans will this spring march up Pennsylvania Avenue, though fifty years late, cheered by the wearers of the blue, and this will be their thought, "Peace on earth and good will to men," one country, one flag, one President; "but memory makes love eternal."

A MOTHER OF THE CONFEDERACY.

BY T. J. MOSLEY, WASHINGTON, D. C.

Mrs. Margaret Fullerton Abney was born near Pickensville, Pickens County, Ala., on October 18, 1829. Her father was one James Fullerton, born of a respectable family in Belfast, Ireland, in the year 1799. He came to America at the age of

MRS. ABNEY AND A LITTLE GREAT-GRANDDAUGHTER.

seventeen, chose the South as the land of his adoption, and when yet a young man found means of bringing his mother, one brother, and three sisters across the ocean to him. Shortly afterwards he was married to Adaline Heflin, a daughter of Alabama. Sons and daughters were born to them, of whom the last survivor is the Margaret of this sketch.

At the age of seventeen Margaret Fullerton became the wife of Paul Collins Abney, a youngster of the same age; for those

were the days when youth wedded on instinct and was blest —days when the joy of life and the call of adventure pulsed with the blood. The young couple at once steered a bold course westward and first settled in Louisiana, where their eldest son was born; two years later found them established in their life home, a delightful seat a mile west of the present town of Lufkin, Angelina County, Tex. There amid the magnolias and the pines they reared a family of nine stalwart sons and three unspoiled daughters, not to mention a sister's three orphaned children—all heirs of God's out-of-doors and the best traditions and ideals of the Old South.

At the outbreak of the War between the States P. C. Abney found himself disqualified for active service on account of an arm crippled in a hunting accident. He therefore continued in his duties as assessor and collector of Texas, at the same time supervising government commissary stores and looking after the interests of the women and children left behind. His part in the war was not the least noble played during those heroic days, as Angelina County can testify.

Meanwhile the eldest son, James Abney, heard with impatience his country's call, but it was not until 1864 that his years qualified him for effective service. But at that earliest possible moment James might have been seen riding away from the pleasant farm home astride his father's strongest horse, a rugged, stout-hearted seventeen-year-old boy. He carried with him two serviceable gray suits, of which he was very proud; for when a mother spins, weaves, cuts, and stitches two suits complete for a fellow, he has every right to consider himself well taken care of. James Abney had a splendid blanket too from the same loom. Neither did he lack for saddle and shoes—there were lots of cowhides, oak bark, and big tanning vats in Angelina County in those days and more people who knew how to get about making shoes and saddles than do at the present time. Consider also that James was further equipped with a tremendously long, hard-kicking rifle and his mother's blessing, and you have a picture of the "Happy Warrior" that Wordsworth himself could not improve. Young Abney was sworn into Capt. H. G. Lane's company, E, Anderson's Regiment, Kirby Smith's division, in March, 1864, and performed efficiently all the duties of a soldier until discharged in June, 1865.

Thus did the dear old lady whose picture is shown on this page earn her title as a "Mother of the Confederacy." To substantiate her claim still further, there is living to-day at Lufkin her son-in-law, E. H. F. McMullen, who celebrated his golden wedding last year and is himself a great-grandfather. He enlisted in the Confederate army as a member of Company D, 7th Texas Cavalry, Sibley's Brigade, better known afterwards as Green's Brigade. He was mustered in at San Antonio in September, 1861, and served throughout the war. Returning safe and sound to the girl he left behind him, he was wedded to Miss Sarah Abney in the fall of 1865.

Mrs. Abney has thirty-nine grandchildren, forty-three great-grandchildren, and one great-great-granddaughter; so that she possesses the unusual distinction of living into the fifth generation. So here you see her sitting at ease in the home of her veteran son at Brownwood, Tex., happy in the company of little Miss Helen Elizabeth Abney, a great-granddaughter. Serenely she looks through her window at the stream of younger life flowing past, rich in memory, plenteous in good deeds, and comforted by the thought that her eighty-seven years have not been without their part in the establishment of the civilization of Texas, the mightiest star in the constellation of the South.

Confederate Veteran.

CAPT. BROMFIELD LEWIS RIDLEY.

A TRIBUTE BY HIS FRIEND AND COMRADE, CAPT. RICHARD BEARD.

Capt. Bromfield L. Ridley, who died at his home, in Murfreesboro, Tenn., on January 12, 1917, was born near the old town of Jefferson, Rutherford County, Tenn., which is now a "deserted village," but in the early life of Tennessee prided itself on being the county seat, having a courthouse and large brick hotel for the accommodation of distinguished visitors. Among those who attended the courts there were Gen. Andrew Jackson, Thomas H. Benton, and a number of other worthies whose names were famous in the early history of the State.

Young Ridley was a playmate and schoolmate of the hero-martyr Sam Davis. They attended a school near Old Jefferson taught by Rufus McClain, of Lebanon, afterwards a captain in the 7th Tennessee Regiment, and were together in the Military Academy at Nashville when the war broke out, from which Sam Davis enlisted in Company I, 1st Tennessee Regiment. Ridley went home and was in the rear of the Federal army when, on the 31st of December, 1862, McCook's Corps, on the right of the Federal line of battle, was shattered by Cleburne's and Cheatham's Divisions. Vast numbers of McCook's command ingloriously left the field and, straggling through woods and cornfields, made their way toward Nashville. "Brom" Ridley and other youngsters from the neighborhood of Jefferson, such as President Davis called the "seed corn of the Confederacy," armed themselves with shotguns and other implements of warfare and captured vast numbers of the stragglers, including a Federal colonel, who was afterwards cashiered for cowardice.

Soon after this young Ridley enlisted in a company of Ward's Regiment, in Morgan's command, his brother, George C. Ridley, being a lieutenant in the company. He had his first baptism of fire in the battle of Milton, Tenn., where Morgan, coming in contact with a largely superior force of the enemy, met with disaster. Ridley was with his captain on the field when the latter fell mortally wounded and begged the boy not to leave him. True to the instincts of a chivalrous nature, the gallant boy picked up the body of his captain, who was dying, if not already dead, and trudged slowly back to his command, which had already retired, knowing that the death-dealing bullets of the enemy were following every step he made.

After this he was commissioned a lieutenant and ordered to duty as aid on the staff of Gen. A. P. Stewart. He was with General Stewart at Chickamauga, all through the Dalton and Atlanta campaign, the ill-starred and ill-fated expedition of Hood into Tennessee in the fall and winter of 1864, and finally at Greensboro, N. C., where, on April 26, 1865, the Southern Confederacy became only a memory. Returning home, he entered a private school, taught in the old university building at Murfreesboro, and later entered the Law Department of Cumberland University, at Lebanon, from which he graduated with honor. He then entered upon the practice of law at Murfreesboro, becoming the junior member of the firm of Ridley and Avent, and from that time he was an active and successful practitioner until his death, accumulating a handsome estate. He was a writer of ability, and some years ago he published his reminiscences of the war under the title of "Campaigns and Battles of the Army of Tennessee." He was well known throughout Rutherford County, and few men have been more missed than he.

Captain Ridley was married on December 4, 1879, to Miss

CAPT. B. L. RIDLEY.

Idelette Lyon, daughter of the Rev. James A. Lyon, D.D., of Columbus, Miss., who survives him with two sons.

His last official act was attaching his notarial seal to an instrument of law for me the evening before he died. We separated then for the last time. The next morning I was shocked to learn that he had died suddenly the night before. Comrade, farewell!

"Sleep deep, sleep in peace, sleep in memory ever;
 Wrapt be the soul in the deeds of its deathless endeavor
 Till the stars be recalled and the firmament furled
 In the dawn of a daylight undying."

THE BATTLE OF YELLOW BAYOU.

During the retreat of Banks's army from its unsuccessful Red River expedition many engagements took place between it and the pursuing Confederate army, under Gen. Richard Taylor. None was more spirited and hotly contested than the battle of Yellow Bayou, which took place on the 18th of April, 1864. The scene of this engagement was along an inland stream, a tributary of Bayou des Glaises, in the eastern section of the parish of Aroyelles, about two miles from the Atchafalaya River. The Federal army, after meeting slight resistance at Marksville, Mansura, and Moreauville, found the Confederates in force ready to meet it and formed in line of battle at Yellow Bayou. General Taylor's command, after the victories of Mansfield and Spring Hill, had, however, been considerably reduced by the transfer of about fifteen thousand of its veteran soldiers to Arkansas to join Gen. Kirby Smith, and there were left him just enough men to harass the retreating Federals. General Polignac, who, after the death of General Mouton at Mansfield, had been promoted to the command of a division, commanded the Louisiana troops and General Walker the Texans, their divisions numbering but a few thousand each.

All along and around Yellow Bayou was a dense wood in which the Confederates were concealed. As soon as the "bluecoats," as Polignac called them, appeared near that now famous bayou the Confederate batteries, notably the St. Mary Cannoneers and the Pelicans of Louisiana and the Benton of Texas, opened a fierce fire and precipitated a deadly conflict between the contending forces which soon became general. The rattle of musketry and the boom of cannon made this hitherto peaceful and fertile valley echo and reëcho with their fearful sounds. The battle began at eleven o'clock in the morning and lasted until four o'clock in the afternoon, when the Confederates withdrew or rather ceased firing and permitted the enemy to pass by on its way to the east side of the Mississippi River.

While the Confederates had but a handful of men against Banks's entire army, the result was decidedly in favor of the boys in gray. There were between 1,200 and 1,500 men killed, the Federals losing about two-thirds of that number. A large number of Avoyelles boys took part in the battle and acquitted themselves, like their comrades in arms, as true heroes. Many were killed, and to-day their kinsmen point with pride to the spot where they met a soldier's death, dying in defense of principles deemed worthy the arbitrament of the sword.

The effect of this engagement was to rid the Trans-Mississippi Department of the army of invasion, and ever afterwards the resounding footsteps and dull tramp of a hostile soldiery ceased to be heard on this side of the Mississippi River. The lesson taught the invaders at Mansfield, Spring Hill, Monette Ferry, and Yellow Bayou was not soon forgotten and caused the armed hosts of the North to leave in peace and tranquillity the valleys of the Red and Atchafalaya.

IN CAMP AND PRISON.

[At the request of his family, the following story of his services as a soldier was dictated by John Rupert Baird in 1910 at his home, in Baird, Miss. He was a native of that State, born at the plantation home of his parents, near Wanalak, Noxubee County, in May, 1841. When he returned from the army, he settled in Sunflower County, where he accumulated a large landed estate and became prominent as a leading citizen. Many years before his death his health failed; but in the midst of his great suffering he was bright and cheerful, always sanguine, genial, and hospitable, interested in all matters of private and public concern. He died at his home, in Columbus, Miss., on August 27, 1916, and was laid to rest in Friendship Cemetery, of that city.

I was at Bethany College, Va., when war was declared and started home at once, going down the Ohio River from Wheeling to Cairo, then down the Mississippi to Vicksburg. Federal troops were then stationed at Cairo. As my father, Dr. James M. Baird, with his family, had refugeed to his plantation in Sunflower County, Miss., to escape the Federals, I went directly there. Soon after I enlisted in Blythe's Mississippi Regiment, Cheatham's Brigade. We went first to Union City, Tenn., and drilled. I was selected as a sharpshooter and placed in the battalion of Maj. William Richards. We next camped for a short while at New Madrid, Mo., going thence to Columbus, Ky., into winter quarters, afterwards dropping back to Union City and vicinity. From there we went to Shiloh, participating in that battle. We then fell back and were transferred to Chattanooga and Stevensonville,

marched through Tennessee into Kentucky, being in General Bragg's army, camped a day or two at Cave City, and had a battle at Mumfordsville in Gen. James Chalmers's brigade. Here Col. William Richards, of Columbus, Miss., and of our battalion of sharpshooters, was shot through the lungs with a Minie ball. I was wounded on the nose, lip, and hand, and lost three teeth by being struck by a fragment of shell.

I went home on a three weeks' furlough, then rejoined my command between Atlanta and Chattanooga, when we marched to Chickamauga and fought there and at Missionary Ridge, where I was captured and kept in prison at Rock Island for nineteen months. I was detailed as a clerk in the adjutant's office, on parole oath, to keep his books, records, etc., and was afterwards detailed in the office of the surgeon in charge as clerk. For this I was paid a small amount and received all the citizen's clothes I needed and many comforts. I was allowed the freedom of the city, also of Moline and Davenport, under parole oath. During this time I made the acquaintance of many Southern sympathizers, known as "Copperheads," and frequently visited Miss Kate P—— and the Misses B——, all of Kentucky. I remained at the prison until all were exchanged, and when ready to return home I was given $25 and furnished transportation to Cairo and thence down the Mississippi River to Greenville. The captain of the boat refused to stop there, but went over to Gaines's Landing, Ark., where I spent the night on a plantation.

The following morning I attempted to cross in a dugout, but was soon compelled to throw the water out vigorously with

JOHN R. BAIRD.

the paddles; and it became a problem as to whether to return or to continue to the Mississippi shore. When about half over, the boat began to sink. I eased myself out, first passing my arm through the handles of my grip, which contained many trinkets for the dear ones at home, such as beautiful pieces of jewelry made by me and other prisoners from rubber combs and other articles and inlaid with shells resembling mother-of-pearl. As the boat turned over I caught the gunnels and rested my chin upon the end which afforded a support. I thus floated for an hour and a half, until I saw a boat coming downstream. When the boat had come near enough, an Irish deck hand threw out an immense rope which struck me across the face and head, but I grasped it. I then held up my grip for him to take, but with an oath he said I was a greenhorn not to let it drop. Finally he reached down, and just as he caught the handles of the grip the rope broke, and it sank out of sight forever. I was in a dazed condition for a while after being taken on board. Fortunately, a Rock Island comrade from Louisiana named Hazzard, who happen to be a passenger, recognized me and procured restoratives which brought me warmth and life, and dry clothing was also provided me. I was landed at Greenville, where I borrowed a mule and soon reached my home in Sunflower County.

SONS OF CONFEDERATE VETERANS

ORGANIZED IN JULY, 1896, AT RICHMOND, VA.

OFFICERS.

Commander in Chief, Ernest G. Baldwin, Roanoke, Va.
Adjutant in Chief, N. B. Forrest, Biloxi, Miss.

MEMBERSHIP CAMPAIGN IN DISTRICT OF COLUMBIA.

BY W. E. BROCKMAN, COMMANDER D. OF C. DIVISION.

A monster membership campaign is now being inaugurated by the Sons in the District of Columbia with the idea of enrolling one thousand Sons by the time of the Reunion in Washington, which has been set for June 5, 6, and 7. Mr. T. Frank Morgan has been made chairman of this committee, and he will start the work in earnest by sending out several thousand letters to those eligible for membership and will also make this appeal through the newspapers.

It now looks as if the Sons would have from five to ten thousand members uniformed to march in the parade. Col. Robert N. Harper, Chairman of the Civic Committee in Washington, is making an appeal to all the cities in the South, through the medium of their Chambers of Commerce, to uniform every Veteran and Son that can be found and, with bands of music, send them on to the national capital as representatives of their city. Dr. Clarence J. Owens, Assistant Adjutant in Chief, is making an appeal to each Camp in the Confederation to send large delegations uniformed to the Reunion.

In order that all visitors may be well cared for and entertained, the city has announced a plan of erecting a structure on the monument grounds that will accommodate any number. Sleeping quarters and free medical attention will be provided for all veterans who desire to make this building their headquarters. In addition to this, all veterans and their families will be provided with free medical attention during their entire stay in this city.

Maj. E. W. R. Ewing, Chairman of the Sons' Reunion Committee, will return at an early date to this city and open the Sons' Reunion headquarters, where all communications for information should be addressed.

COMMANDER OF THE TENNESSEE DIVISION.

Commander in Chief Ernest G. Baldwin has announced the appointment of R. I. McClearen, of Nashville, Tenn., as Commander of the Tennessee Division, succeeding Walter C. Chandler, of Memphis. Mr. McClearen is one of the active young business men of Nashville and has been prominently identified with the Sons of Confederate Veterans for several years, serving as Commander of the Third Brigade on the staff of Commander Chandler.

Tennessee is divided into six Brigades, and upon each Commander rests the active work of organizing new Camps and making preparations for reunions. Commander McClearen is now selecting his Brigade Commanders to perfect the State official organization. His staff will be composed of about eighteen members of the organization in various parts of the State. It is hoped to make Tennessee lead in the number of Camps and members to report at the Washington Reunion in June. General activity along this line has begun in all parts of the South.

"COMMODORE MONTGOMERY"—A CORRECTION.

BY W. F. CLAYTON FLORENCE, ALA.

In the VETERAN for January, 1917, appears an article by Mrs. Eloise Tyler Jacobs, Historian of the Illinois Division, U. D. C., giving a history of Commodore Montgomery, whom she styles a "naval hero." It appears that this article is taken from the Chicago Tribune of April 5, 1896; therefore she is not to blame for its being mostly fiction.

As Secretary of the Survivors' Association of the Confederate States Navy, it is my duty to keep the record of that branch of the Confederacy straight. We simply want facts; our record needs no embellishment. It stands for itself when truthfully told.

Montgomery was never in the Confederate States navy; as to his connection with the army I know nothing. He was a kind of "water rover," subject to no authority other than to do the enemy all the harm he could. He organized a small fleet of river boats and operated mostly in or on the upper Mississippi River. Like Mosby and Morgan, he did considerable damage to the enemy. His daring attracted much comment and praise, but his career was short, continuing only until the United States was able to build a Mississippi fleet, when he was driven up rivers flowing into the Mississippi where the United States boats could not pursue. I don't wish to detract from his record, for while it lasted it showed him to be a man of extraordinary courage and ability and one of whom the Confederacy was proud. My object is only to keep the record straight.

Commodore Montgomery was not the inventor of what is termed here as the "submarine ram." It was as old as the hills, consisting only of a mere pointed piece of iron placed on the bow of the ship to strengthen the bow and protect it in case of a collision. Neither did he fit one to the warship Virginia (Merrimac). I was an eye-witness of the Hampton Roads naval battle, being a midshipman on the Patrick Henry, which participated in the Saturday's fight on March 8, 1862, on which day the Cumberland was sunk by the Virginia, and in striking her the submarine ram, as here styled, was wrenched off. That was the only ship the Virginia ever rammed. Nor did this claimed invention inspire the building of the Monitor, as she arrived at Fortress Monroe Saturday night, and the battle with the Virginia took place on Sunday, March 9, 1862. Neither did he file charges against Commodore Hollins or they were thrown in the wastebasket, for Hollins was the officer who bombarded Greytown for an insult to our flag before the war and who, with an army officer, Colonel Thomas, of Baltimore, captured the steamer St. Nicholas running between Baltimore and Washington, D. C.

A story of this capture will not be out of place here. Hollins conceived the idea of capturing this boat; so, immediately running alongside the United States gunboat Pawnee, the largest of the Potomac fleet, under the plea of having mail for her, he captured her and others of the United States fleet. Certainly a daring proposition. He then sent Thomas to Baltimore, who there disguised himself as a woman and took passage for Washington under the name of Madame Zarvona. She had several large trunks and on the way down, complaining of the headache, retired to her stateroom. At every stopping place laborers were boarding the steamer, going to Washington to hunt work, and when the boat reached Point Lookout a venerable old man took passage for Washington. The steamer had barely cleared the wharf when the lady came from her stateroom dressed as a Confederate officer, the old man threw off his disguise, and the laborers opened the trunks containing arms. The surprised captain surrendered without resistance. No United States gunboats being in the vicinity, Hollins's plan to capture the Pawnee failed; but he overhauled several ships and burned them, then, running up the Rappahanock River, dismantled and burned the St. Nicholas. Does such an act show cowardice? The only Confederate ship on the upper Mississippi that made any special record was the Arkansas.

Montgomery had nothing to do with raising or converting the Merrimac into a war vessel; Confederate States naval officers did that. The claim of sinking the Preble as captain of the Van Dorn is entirely fiction. I have before me the United States naval list of vessels that attacked New Orleans after bombarding Fort Jackson for several days, and the Preble is not in the list; neither is the Van Dorn in the list of the Confederate fleet.

The naval records of both the United States and Confederate States mention nothing of Montgomery in the fights between the Arkansas and the Federal fleet, and all that is claimed for him in this article is fiction, for his claim to sinking the United States Mound City fairly contradicts the story. After the destruction of the Arkansas, her officers and crew were transferred to land batteries. Capt. Joseph Fry, who commanded the Confederate States steamer Haurepas, escaped to White River. Hearing that the enemy's fleet was coming up to assist General Curtis, Fry ran his vessel a short distance below St. Charles, sank his ship and two others to prevent their passage, and placed his men and guns in two batteries, he commanding one and Lieutenant Dunnington the other. On June 17, 1862, the Mound City, St. Louis, Lexington, and Connestoga appeared and opened fire upon him. Fry waited until he had the Mound City between the two batteries, then both batteries opened upon her; a shot entered her boilers and blew her up.

Montgomery claims that he built the great man-of-war Nashville which sank seven of Farragut's fleet one morning. Was there ever such rot published? The ironclad Tennessee and the wooden gunboats Morgan, Gaines, and Selma constituted the Confederate fleet at Mobile when Farragut with his fleet attacked. The Tennessee carried six guns, Commander J. D. Johnson; the Gaines, six guns, Capt. G. W. Harrison; the Selma, four guns, Capt. P. Murphy. Farragut's fleet consisted of four monitors, with fourteen wooden ships carrying one hundred and forty-eight guns of large caliber. The Confederates lost the Tennessee, while the Federals lost the monitor Tecumseh, with her whole crew, between four hundred and five hundred men and officers. The whole loss of the Confederates was: killed, 12; wounded, 19. The Federals, killed, 172; wounded, 112, or more than all of Buchanan's command. The Tennessee, having had her steering gear shot away, became unmanageable and in that position was surrounded by the Federal fleet at short range, when Buchanan, commander of the fleet, surrendered, as did also the Selma. The Morgan escaped to the city of Mobile. Thus ended the battle of Mobile, which occurred on August 5, 1864.

At Mobile Captain Ferrand had on the stocks two ironclads building and the wooden steamers Nashville, Baltic, and Morgan. The approaches to Mobile had been pretty well protected by torpedoes, and after the evacuation of the forts the Yankees turned their attention to the city; but before they got it they lost another monitor and seven wooden ships. The city was occupied by the Federals on April 11, 1865.

I might analyze this fairy tale in which Montgomery is "Jack the giant killer" to its whole length, but nothing more is necessary. I want to say that I don't place any of the blame on Mrs. Jacobs, but on the Chicago Tribune. I am confident that its information never came from the lips of Commodore Montgomery, whose record exonerates him from such froth and self-praise; and it is simply to keep the record straight that I ask for this correction.

MY BIRTHDAY.

BY W. H. KEARNEY, TREZEVANT, TENN.

To-day, the 9th of January, 1917, I am made to realize that life, like the natural day, has its morning, noon, and evening, its joys and its sorrows, and that the aged cannot feel the exhilarating brightness of life. For I am celebrating my seventy-third anniversary to-day. Many changes have come in those seventy-three years. The old-fashioned fireplace, the stagecoach, the spinning wheel and hand loom have all disappeared for things more convenient.

My memory runs back to about fifty-five years ago, to March, 1862. I was only eighteen years old, dreaming of a bright future, when war came as a bolt out of the blue. Then I quit dreaming and went to face the cruel and bitter realities of war. I joined Company L, of the 6th Tennessee Regiment, and on the 27th of June, 1862, we fought a great battle at Dead Angle, Ga., and slaughtered many. Oftentimes we were very tired and hungry, and after a long, cold journey we would wrap ourselves in our blankets and lie down to sleep all night, awaking the next morning to find ourselves buried in the snow. I was wounded in the battle of Chickamauga, but, being only a flesh wound, it didn't delay me very long. I was also in the last battle fought at Nashville, December 15 and 18, 1864. We endured many hardships during those four years. Memory fails me when I try to recall them all, but I do remember that I went home without any shoes upon my feet.

Most of the comrades with whom I started have one by one gone on before; two of those I loved last year, Capt. W. W. Fulsom, of Hope, Ark., and Dr. W. J. W. Kerr, of Corsicana, Tex.

Long may the CONFEDERATE VETERAN live in its noble work! It will ever be a welcome visitor in my home.

A WEAK LINK.

A Connecticut man who says he was a spy for the Union army at the time of our late family row was over in Atlanta a day or so ago and while there told the newspaper boys some of the thrilling experiences he had while Sherlocking in that immediate vicinity. Among other things, he said: "I came into Atlanta in '62, slipping into the Confederate lines to see what I could. Somebody got next to me, and while I was trying to get away I heard bloodhounds baying. I was away out near the river then, and I beat them to it and got out in the water up to my knees. The hounds came on in single file. I was afraid to use my revolver because of the noise, but had a big knife, and as each hound leaped for my throat I caught him by the neck with my left hand and stabbed him to the heart with my knife. I dropped all six of them into the river and swam across." Which would be thrilling enough if it were not that, for us anyway, the edge had been taken off by seeing it in "The Life of Ananias" or somewhere before it appeared in the Atlanta papers.—*Macon Telegraph.*

Training the dogs so they would come at him one at a time must have been the hardest part of the feat.—*Mobile Register.*

MANASSAS BATTLE FIELD PARK.

BY GEORGE C. ROUND, MANASSAS, VA.

About fifteen years ago a bill was introduced into Congress by our member, Hon. John M. Piney, to provide for the care and preservation of the monuments and other historical associations connected with the first battle field of the War between the States and the field nearest the capital of the nation. Since that time the Military Committee of the House has given hearings to the veterans on both sides who favor the project and to the Daughters of the Confederacy, who have erected near Groveton a white marble monument in the Confederate Cemetery and near by a pretty pavilion in which excursion parties of both gray and blue have been at various times welcomed. The various hearings were printed in a House document three years ago, together with the report made by the War Department at the request of Congress.

Our present member of Congress, Hon. C. C. Carlin, introduced a year ago House Bill No. 8 to carry out the recommendations of the Army Board and hopes to secure favorable action at the present Congress. Finding that the House document which contained the hearings mentioned and the map from the War Department was not obtainable at the present time owing to the great demand therefor, Mr. Carlin has secured a reprint of two thousand copies. This letter is written to suggest that the VETERAN readers who are interested write at once to their members of Congress asking for a copy of Mr. Carlin's bill, No. 8, Sixty-Fourth Congress, and House document No. 481, Sixty-Third Congress, second session. It is important to mention the Sixty-Third Congress, as the report in question was made three years ago. This document contains much interesting historical matter only obtainable therefrom. I also ask your interested readers to write their members to interview Mr. Carlin and to assure him of their support for his bill.

The report of the Army Board recommends the purchase by the United States of one hundred and twenty-eight acres of the Henry farm and one hundred and forty-five acres of the Dogan farm. It may be of interest to know that these tracts of land are both still in the possession of the same families owning them in 1861 and 1862.

The writer is a subscriber to the VETERAN and is known to many of its readers as a Union signal officer during the war who settled at Manassas in the practice of law in 1869. He is vain enough to ask your readers to read the "Brief" filed with the Army Board and published on pages 5-11 of said House document No. 481 of the Sixty-Third Congress, in which he has endeavored to bring out some singular facts regarding these historic plains with which the history of our country is so closely identified.

In closing I venture to refer to the dedication by Northern and Southern veterans on September 30 of last year of a jubilee tablet on our courthouse lawn, corner of Grant and Lee Avenues. The tablet is part of a striking commemorative group erected by our County Board of Supervisors, consisting of two bronze cannon of the vintage of 1862 and other military and naval insignia secured for us from the United States Congress by Mr. Carlin. The unique inscription is as follows:

"In commemoration of the Manassas National Jubilee of Peace, the first instance in history where suvivors of a great battle met fifty years after and exchanged friendly greetings at the place of actual combat. Here on July 21, 1911, the closing scene was enacted."

"The tableau of the reunited States. The President, the Governor of Virginia, and forty-eight maidens in white took part with 1,000 veterans of the blue and the gray and 10,000 citizens of the new America."

At the time of the great Confederate Reunion in Washington next spring I shall be glad to join in welcoming the boys in gray to these historic and battle-scarred plains.

TO YOU AND ALL YOUR FAMILY.

Al Field, leader in the minstrel world, is a philosopher as well as fun-maker. His "Tenth Annual Letter to Bill Brown," sent out as a Christmas and New Year greeting "to all mankind," is invigorating by its breeziness. Now and then he drops into verse that "helps to point a moral." He says:

"Life is a short day's climb, and it behooves us to make the best of it for our fellow men's sake.

"There is only one method of meeting life's test—
Just keep on a-strivin' and hope for the best;
Don't give up the ship and retire in dismay
'Cause hammers are thrown when you'd like a bouquet.
This world would be tiresome, we'd all get the blues
If all the folks in it held the same views.
So finish your work, show the best of your skill;
Some people won't like it, but other folks will.

If you're leading an army or building a fence,
Do the best that you kin with your own common sense.
One small word of praise in this journey of tears
Outweighs in the balance 'gainst a cartload of sneers.
The plants that we're passing as commonplace weeds
Oft prove to be jes' what the sufferer needs.
So keep on a-goin'; don't you stay standin' still;
Some people won't like you, but other folks will."

He heartily subscribes to this New Year resolution: "We agree to let the unfortunate past drop into oblivion and never recall a disagreeable mistake unless it be to arm ourselves against falling into further error.

"So here's to the coming year—
A prayer, a song, a cry,
To the God of passing years,
Who can give us strength for the journey's length
And rainbow all our tears."

COLONEL OF 5TH TENNESSEE CAVALRY.—W. G. Allen, of Dayton, Tenn., calls attention to an error by Dr. Donoho in his article on "A Long Night," page 27 of the January VETERAN, in referring to a "Colonel McKinley" as commanding some Tennessee cavalry. Mr. Allen says: "Gen. W. Y. C. Hume's division, composed of Terrell's and Ashby's Brigades of Cavalry, covered the W. & A. Railroad from Dalton to Atlanta. The battle of Calhoun was fought May 16, 1864. Col. George W. McKenzie commanded the 5th Tennessee Cavalry, of Ashby's Brigade, which was Wheeler's rear guard in posting pickets. I was adjutant of the 5th Tennesese, and I came by the field hospital, where the wounded were left. After hearing a report of wounded being left, Colonel McKenzie directed me to write an order to Dr. Delany, Ashby's Brigade surgeon, for ambulances to carry the wounded to a place of safety. I remember well talking to the comrades and wounded, but don't remember the names. Those were busy days and nights. I have the old order book of the 5th Regiment. There was no Colonel McKinley in Hume's Division or Wheeler's Corps. If there is an adjutant of Hume's Division now living, I would like to hear from him."

[In a list of officers of the Confederate army there is no one by the name of McKinley; so it is evident that the officer referred to by Dr. Donoho was Col. George W. McKenzie, of the 5th Tennessee Cavalry.]

On page 549 of the December VETERAN an error in title of article locates the battle of Dingle's Mill in Florida instead of in South Carolina.

In the article by John W. Higgins, on page 78, sixteenth line from bottom of column, there is reference to "engaging McLoud's army," when it should have been "McClellan's."

INFORMATION WANTED.—Mr. Leroy S. Boyd, 15 Seventh Street N. E., Washington, D. C., desires to hear from any one who knows anything about the Kappa Alpha College Fraternity, which existed at many Southern colleges before the war and which died out in 1866. It was also called Kuklos Adelphon, or Circle of Brothers. Its badge was diamond-shaped, with a large circle in the center and the letter "A" in the center of the circle. Names of members especially desired and location of chapters.

Mrs. E. S. Crowell, of Chelsea, Mass., wishes to secure the record of her grandfather, John Floyd Stallings, as a Confederate soldier. He enlisted from Mississippi and served in the artillery; at one time he was under General Bragg. She will appreciate hearing from any of his surviving comrades.

Mrs. E. L. Dickenson, of Herndon, Ky., Route 1, is anxious to get in communication with some one who remembers her husband, R. D. Dickenson, who was with Captains Craig and Nelson under Generals Forrest and Bell. His duty was to gather up the cattle and deliver to the commissary department.

John W. Bratcher, of Mena, Ark., wants to get in communication with some one who can testify to the service of James P. Hasty, who enlisted in Company A, 28th Tennessee Regiment of Infantry, in 1861 under Capt. Parker Simms and Col. John P. Murray. Mr. Hasty was wounded in the battle of Murfreesboro and discharged. He afterwards joined the 16th Tennessee Regiment, Company B, commanded by Ad Fisk. He also would like to hear from some one who knew J. H. Parker, of the 31st Tennessee Infantry and 12th Tennessee consolidated. The widows of these men are in need of pensions.

THE JEFFERSON DAVIS MEMORIAL.
(Continued from page 56.)

Julian S. Carr, of North Carolina, has made this possible. It will be a magnificent memorial not only to Mr. Davis, but to the Confederate States, for it will be the most imposing of all the monuments which have been erected to the glory of Southern manhood and womanhood. This great work will certainly interest many people throughout the Southland who would be glad to contribute in some amount to the completion of the wonderful monument.

Capt. John H. Leathers, Treasurer of the Jefferson Davis Home Association, Louisville, Ky., reports that $2,000 was received during the month. All contributions should be sent to him. Everybody is asked to contribute liberally.

R. U. Brown, of Lytle, Tex., enlisted in the Confederate service on the 22d of May, 1861, at Jackson, Tenn., in a company commanded by Captain Haywood, later merged in the 7th Tennessee Cavalry Regiment. He would like to hear from some of his old comrades.

Marion W. Ripy, Inter-Southern Life Building, Louisville, Ky., is trying to complete the record of George Washington Brown. It is thought that he served under Captain Fitzhenry until his death and then under Captain Buchanan. He was with Forrest. His widow is in need of a pension.

Mrs. I. L. Newsome, 606 East Houston Avenue, Marshall, Tex., wants information of the service of her husband, I. L. Newsome, who enlisted at Sebastopol, Miss., and was under Captain Howard; second lieutenant, Hardy Hill. They were at Jackson, Miss., two months. He was in the Bethel fight.

Mrs. J. K. Munnerlyn, of Jacksonville, Fla., wishes to hear from any one who can testify to the record of Capt. W. D. Olivieros, who entered the Confederate service in Company B, 8th Georgia Regiment, was later transferred to the navy, and was commander of the steamer Resolute at the time she was tender to Ram Savannah. Captain Olivieros is eighty-four years of age and is in need of a pension.

Mrs. Edward Schaaf, of St. Mary's, Mo., is trying to complete the record of her uncle, William Henry Harrison Cox, known as Harry Cox, who enlisted in the Confederate army early in 1862 from Pocahontas, Ark., and served until the end of the war. His brother, George Washington Cox, also enlisted in the 7th Arkansas under General Shaver. He was made lieutenant at Corinth. Any information of either will be gladly received.

D. F. Thompson, of Jefferson City, Mo., seeks information of one Rev. James C. Thompson, who at the beginning of the war was a resident of Dunklin County, Mo., and presiding elder of the Bloomfield Circuit, Methodist Episcopal Church, South. He was chaplain of an Arkansas regiment—thinks it was the 45th Arkansas Infantry Volunteers —and died a few months after his return from the war. Information is wanted of his life and where he is buried.

Dr. Milton Dunn, of Aloha, La., makes inquiry for W. M. Ettor, a native of Virginia and a jeweler by trade, who, when Virginia seceded, left Montgomery, La., and volunteered with the troops from that State.